MOTHER OF THE NATION: CLARA EVANS MUHAMMAD

Wife of Elijah Muhammad, Mother of Imam W. Deen Mohammed (The Latter Years: 1930 -1972)

Dr. R. Zakiyyah Muhammad

ISBN: 9798846551978

To the family of Clara and Elijah Muhammad, with special thanks to Dr. Akbar Muhmmad (1939-2016)

To our mothers - past, present, and future - and the men who honor them.

CONTENTS

(James Baldwin, Malcolm X, Louis X, and Muham

FOREWORD

I wonder how many Black Americans owe their sensibilities, their self-esteem and success to a quiet, slender, dark woman who grew up in humble circumstances in rural Georgia at the dawn of the 20th century?

As I write this, Richard Williams, the father of tennis stars Venus and Serena Williams, is being honored for his ability to mold the characters of two gifted individuals, so they could train, excel and blossom both physically and intellectually, and become wealthy and influential celebrities.

But as the late Dr. R. Zakiyyah Muhammad shows in this far-ranging biography, Clara Evans Muhammad, the "Mother" of the Nation of Islam, in concert with her husband, the Honorable Elijah Muhammad, fortified the minds and hearts and bolstered the achievements of millions of Black people in the USA and beyond over the last three or so generations.

Islam, in the evolving forms in which they conceived it, served the Muhammads as an instrument with which to lift up people who otherwise were most likely to wallow in self-doubt, if not self-hatred, condemned to live as victims confused and confounded by societal forces that continually assaulted and plagued their life-chances from cradle to grave.

Today, according to the Pew Research Center, there are more than 4.5 million Muslims in the USA. Of the 1.5 million or so who have been in this country for three or more generations, the majority are Black, and the NOI is acknowledged to be the greatest influence on this segment by far. The Black Americans who descended from Africans enslaved here centuries ago are the native seeds upon which the flourishing of this major religion in North America most likely depends.

Yet in mainstream society, people of all colors and backgrounds have been conditioned to think that the Nation of Islam (NOI), the so-called "Black Muslims," have been inspired mainly by hatred and are focused mainly on separating themselves from whites or from Christians of whatever hue. Little if any curiosity is shown to how the NOI developed the means to print and publish an international newspaper and to establish farms, restaurants, supermarkets, fisheries, bakeries and other businesses. Or how it inspired so many members to enter the professions and the arts, or to follow paths to high academic status or to open new dimensions of theological inquiry.

Most movies and other cultural products, whether popular or elite, routinely depict the "Black Muslims" as fanatics worthy of ridicule or contempt. Why this is so I trust you, the honest reader, will answer in your own way as you read this book. But any objective review of how the Muhammads have been represented will show that Elijah has been routinely vilified and Clara all but ignored.

The volume you now hold, unusual in its breadth and in its interweaving of impressively diverse - and sometimes quirky - supportive material, reminds me of the writings of the great 17th century English Christian writer and polymath, Sir Thomas Browne. Like Browne's *Religio Medici*, this book deserves a wide readership and recognition as a classic text. The author, with great passion, deep knowledge and a mighty style, embraces many fields: world and religious history, U.S. history, Black Americana and especially women's history. That scope and originality is what the world wants in a classic text.

Here is a thrilling saga that lifts the veil that has shrouded Clara's life. It depicts her childhood in Cordele, Georgia, when Jim Crow educational practices cut off her formal education. It recounts her romance and elopement with Elijah Poole, against the wishes of her parents, who considered him an unworthy prospect since his family was even poorer than theirs. It follows the youthful Pooles in the Great Migration that took them to Detroit in the mid-1920s, where they lived in a rat-infested slum while Elijah bounced from job to job and Clara, now the young mother of a growing family, supplemented their income with domestic work.

Elijah, frustrated by the poor job opportunities and prevailing bigotry that blighted the lives of most Black citizens, fell into near-suicidal alcoholic despair. But one day, Clara's friend Lula Spell told her of an itinerant foreign preacher who was proclaiming in his Teachings that Black people not only had a past rich with dignity and achievements but also possessed a potential to revive those attributes if only they freed their minds from the mental chains that remained as the most persistent vestige of slavery.

For Clara, it was not so much a matter of *"Stand by your man"* as *"Lift up your man and prop him up."* It was Clara who took Elijah to his fateful introduction to W. D. Fard Muhammad after she had heard the Teachings first. It was Clara who was soon nurturing and shielding her family after Elijah, now a young leader of the NOI, was forced to move from city to city to escape assassination by rivals.

It was Clara who nurtured her seven children while Elijah served a four-year federal prison sentence for refusing to register for the draft. It was Clara who organized the translation and transcription of the Qur'an into English, handwriting the scriptures, along with other women she organized, chapter by chapter. And it was Clara who then defended her Constitutional right to provide the texts to her husband and also the right of prisoners whom he was converting to have access to non-Christian religious works.

It was Clara who resisted attempts to jail her for keeping her children out of inferior public schools in Chicago and to home-school them rather than subject them to a racist curriculum imposed by racist teachers and administrators. It was Clara who pioneered the founding of the NOI's Islamic schools that have fostered high academic aspirations, expectations and effort in their students - a sharp contrast with the low standards and achievement levels in the vast majority of schools in Black neighborhoods.

And finally it was Clara who fortified and inspired her seventh child, Wallace, to become the profound humanitarian sage and leader Warith Deen Mohammed. His death at 75 was a loss for world society because he was a uniter and inspirer, a bold thinker and effective builder of ties between people of good faith and healthful intentions.

Let me close on a personal note. When I met Elijah and Clara Muhammad in 1968, I was about to turn 27 and hoping to join the staff of *Muhammad Speaks* newspaper. I've written about my experiences there elsewhere in my essay, "Messaging the Blackman," which I invite interested readers to find online (if they can overcome efforts to suppress or expunge it), or in the collection *Voices From the Underground* (Incredible Librarian Books, 1993); or in the University of Michigan's journal Voices of the African Diaspora, vol. vii, no. 3, (where it was given the lame title "Testing America's Promise of Free Speech: Muhammad Speaks in the 1960s, A Memoir").

I served as executive editor of Muhammad Speaks for the last three of my four years there and was in Clara Muhammad's presence on only a few occasions, perhaps twice at the family's home and the others while attending Saviour's Day. Although I am not and have never been a Muslim, I will say only that the charisma that Dr. Muhammad's biography discloses in Clara Evans Muhammad's aura was apparent and almost palpable, as others attest throughout this book. She spoke little except around intimates. She was watchful. You felt her gaze on you, a constant appraisal that was also an encouragement for you not to disappoint her expectations. Clara Evans Muhammad's actions were her language, and we are all fortunate that Dr. R. Zakiyyah Muhammad could translate them into a book for the ages.

John Woodford
Ann Arbor, Michigan, USA
March 31, 2022

INTRODUCTION

The Poole family migrated from Georgia to Detroit in 1923 with dreams of economic prosperity. Instead, they faced a city unable to provide its growing population and the onset of the Great Depression. In 1929, Clara found herself on the brink of starvation and struggling to provide for her five young children, including a newborn. Her husband, Elijah Poole, could not keep steady employment and struggled with mental depression and alcohol addiction. He was frequently absent from the home, leaving Clara to tend to the children and find any resources she could to survive.

During the summer of 1930, a beacon of hope appeared in Clara's neighbor, Lula Spell. Lula had recently attended a meeting led by a man who declared the greatness of colored people in a way she had never heard before. His words profoundly affected her, and Lula invited Clara to attend a future meeting. All family members interviewed shared that Clara said out loud, "Maybe he can help my husband."[3]

Clara optimistically intended for Elijah to accompany her and Lula, but Elijah could not be found initially and was in no condition to go when he reappeared. Nevertheless, excited about the prospects, Clara went to the meeting with Lula Spell to hear this mysterious man speak. It was a public meeting overflowing with people, held at 3408 Hastings Street over the Castle Theater in Detroit. When they entered the meeting hall, Clara was immediately transfixed by the words she heard. She was 31 years old and pregnant with her sixth child when she listened to the life-changing message of W. D. Fard Muhammad. Fard was the founder and leader of an organization called *The Lost Found Nation of Islam in the Wilderness of North America*. The Teachings were taught in a place called the Temple or Temple of Islam, and the new Muslims, eventually followers of her husband, were called the Temple People.

The Teachings presented an outline for empowerment and enlightenment. Society, directly and indirectly, told Black people daily that they were cursed and less than all other people. These same individuals were being taught that they were kings and queens stolen from another land. Clara's family had modest resources but lived a comfortable life. She only experienced poverty after she married. Surrounded by educated, refined people, she could draw from her religious background and her education from her school teachers, who taught her that Blacks in the Bible were dignified in history. When Clara's neighbor talked about the glory of Black people, she wondered if such teachings could help her husband.

Clara's response to The Teaching was action. Fard told her during their first encounter, "The next time you come, bring your husband," which she did. She was inspired, even ecstatic, about her encounter with Fard, but Clara's eyes were on Elijah and how The Teachings might affect him. When Elijah finally heard the message of Fard, he was able to overcome the vices that had a grip on him for years. The more Clara learned from The Teachings, the stronger she and her family became. The burden she and the new Muslims carried appeared to be lifted when it became clear that the Black man and woman were not only right with G-D but that G-D had sent someone to them to relieve their burdens.

W. D. Fard Muhammad, through *The Lost Found Nation of Islam in the Wilderness of North America,* introduced a new religion, Islam, with different scriptural text, The Qur'an. It provided an alternative theology and a rationale that elevated the narrative of a people from the bottom to the originators of civilization. After introducing her husband to The Teachings, not only did Clara embrace this religion called Islam, she also worked with her husband, soon-to-be-named Elijah Muhammad, to establish it in the United States of America. The result was in 1931, a door to Islam for Black people opened.

W. D. Fard Muhammad and Clara's husband Elijah eventually developed a close relationship. Fard taught Elijah daily, and Clara was consistently a part of the instruction. Due to her pregnancy with her sixth child, she primarily remained at home, but Fard would frequently visit the family, teaching into the night and often all night. Additionally, Fard taught Clara directly on critical matters relating to women, motherhood, and marriage. When Fard established the Muslim Girls Training and General Civilization Class (MGT&GCC), Clara was the one he officially instructed as to the first MGT. He gave her knowledge and enabled her to teach her daughters, other women, and girls. Furthermore, Clara guided the Nation of Islam's education program, the University of Islam.

When Fard considered leaders for the Nation of Islam, he did not simply look at Elijah. The author believes he looked for a pair, a couple – male and female – who could address the complete needs of the new Nation. Part of that consideration was to select one with a devoted mate to be a dependable support system. This strengthens my position that Fard not only chose Elijah, he also chose Clara. For Clara Evans Poole becoming Muslim was exciting but natural. It was not complex or foreign. It was common sense. It represented the best practice of living one's life with integrity. With her knowledge, training, and leadership, she became one of the most influential women in American history.

This book continues to shed light on the life of Clara Evans Muhammad and the racial and religious transformations that occurred during her lifetime.

PREFACE

Research Process

Multiple interviews were conducted with all of Clara Muhammad's living children, Nathaniel, Elijah, Jr., Lottie Rayya, Dr. Akbar, Imam W. Deen Mohammed, her grandchildren, nephews, and others in person and via telephone. Unfortunately, I did not interview Emmanuel (1921-1998), Ethel Muhammad Sharrieff (1922–2002), or Herbert/Jabir Muhammad (1929–2008).

Questionnaires were used in each interview, and all interviews were recorded, transcribed, and re-checked with the respondents. It was necessary to listen to multiple respondents regarding specific issues to ascertain the recurrent threads in their responses. We discovered several myths had been passed on through the decades. Not having the opportunity to personally interview Clara Muhammad intensified the effort to capture that internal spark that lights a person's soul. That unique self is often represented in quotes, patterns, and phrases one uses.

Throughout the research, visits were made to Cordele, Unadilla, Macon, Detroit, and Atlanta with support and special thanks to Harriet Muhammad-Abu-Bakr. Support staff in Chicago and Washington, D.C. also assisted. The area where Clara lived and the school she attended were studied and the Cordele Public Library where she could not learn. Librarians were interviewed and archives researched. The oldest citizen in Cordele and teachers, principals, and activists who knew the area's history were interviewed. Burnsteen Muhammad, Clara's sister-in-law and secretary to W. D. Fard Muhammad, was interviewed by telephone in 1982 and 2001, the year before she passed.

I interviewed the then oldest member of the Nation of Islam, Mother Ruby Muhammad and Minister Louis Farrakhan, Imam Darnell Karim, and his wife Gloria Karim, whose mother, Viola Kareem, was Clara's close friend and confidant. They offered invaluable contributions. Also, I spoke with Osman Sharief Al Manza, son of original members from 1930. Additional interviews included Mary and Henry Al Manza and Elizabeth Shabazz, widow of Jeremiah Shabazz, who cared for Clara's father in their home.

Use of Terms

The identity of oppressed people is reflected in the terms used to describe them. Kidnapped from Africa in the 1500s, a people were enslaved in the Americas and called a series of dehumanizing names for 400 years: coon, ape, sambo, jungle bunny, pickaninny, savage, jig-a-boo, darkie, spook, and nigger.[1] After Lincoln's Emancipation Proclamation of 1863, the name-calling continued. Still, newly freed people sought to elevate themselves by self-naming (i.e., "slaves and animals are named by their master – free men and women name themselves"). This biography references the terms formerly enslaved have used throughout their unprecedented 400-year search for identity – Colored, Negro, Black, African-American, and Bilalian. The term "Caucasian" is used (with reservation) rather than "white" to describe people of European descent.

Islam, Al-Islam, Othodox, and Sunni Muslim

The term Islam was used during the period 1930 to 1975. When Clara Muhammad's son, Imam W. Deen Mohammed, became the leader in 1975, he introduced the proper term from The Qur'an – Al-Islam. He also rejected the term orthodox Islam and the sectarian labels of Sunni and Shia used by Orientalists. He preferred to define his supporters as seeking to demonstrate the *Uswaah* (character) of Prophet Muhammad (prayers and peace be upon him). As such, he told his supporters, the majority of the Nation of Islam, who followed his father, "We are not to align with *any* foreign government, Muslim or other. We only support the good they do. We are *never* to forget that no government came to our rescue during our nearly 400 years of enslavement and oppression."[2]

When the name Prophet Muhammad or Prophet Muhammad ibn Abdullah is mentioned, "PPBUH" follows, which means, Prayers and Peace Be Upon Him. The spelling of G-D is out of respect for the Divine. Several religious traditions use it to avoid the abuse of reversing the word to dog.

Variations in Spelling of Names

Original Arabic names given to early Muslims were spelled via English transliteration (i.e., Sharrieff). As future generations of Muslims acquired knowledge of the Arabic language, names were spelled consistent with the Arabic (i.e., Sharif). Thus, the variation of names can be seen in the spelling of later generations.

PART 3: MOTHER LEADERSHIP

CHAPTER 1: THE TRADITION OF MOTHER LEADERSHIP

Clara Muhammad was of the tradition of mothers who fought for their families with sheer determination, limited resources, and an abundance of love. This distinctive fight is part of the continuum of Black mothers up from slavery. She was not an activist, feminist or womanist and did not need or want any other term than mother to describe her actions or behavior. Her agency came from her innate connection to The Creator and the mission she believed she had been called to serve. Clara was a woman of faith who stood her ground and navigated the space she occupied. All of her actions were embodied in the roles of *Wife* and *Mother*.

Like the foremothers who preceded her, Clara had the courage of Harriet Tubman, the direct straight talk of Sojourner Truth, and the intelligence and elegance of Anna Julia Cooper. Like Mary McCloud Bethune, Clara Muhammad pressed for quality education for all Black children. From 1932 into the present day, her legacy has continued in the Clara Muhammad Elementary and Secondary Schools.

As a leader of Muslim women in the Muslim Girls Training and General Civilization Class (MGT&GCC), she brought refinement and grace comparable to that Dr. Charlotte Hawkins Brown brought to her finishing school. Clara was as tenacious about the survival of the Nation of Islam as Fannie Lou Hamer and Ella Baker were about justice and the Civil Rights Movement. These great women sought freedom for their people, respect for the Black man and woman, social justice, and quality education within the oppressive social constructs of America. These historical female figures made significant progress in moving America forward toward the ideals it claims are embedded in its

DR. R. ZAKIYYAH MUHAMMAD

foundation.

But, in 1933, Clara Muhammad pioneered a unique construct to the struggle, a new identity for Black women. Fostered by a reconnection to Al-Islam, the ancestral religion torn from Africans during enslavement, Clara exemplified a new perception of self and the world. Albeit Islam via the Nation of Islam was not the full expression of universal Al-Islam consistent in all respects with The Qur'an and the traditions of Prophet Muhammad ibn Abdullah (PPBUH). Nevertheless, it sufficiently reintroduced enough Islamic principles to destroy the root of inferiority that Black people suffered in America: 1) that G-D was white, 2) that Blacks were cursed, 3) that the Bible was historical fact, and 4) that slavery was a result of Blacks inferiority. The work of the *Lost Found Nation of Islam* challenged each of those narratives that have underpinned racism in America and the world.

Clara functioned from a position of independent thinking from the dominant society. Her worldview of freedom, justice, and equality was intellectually and spiritually outside of the framework of Christian thought and Caucasian authority. It was uniquely Islamic, comprehensive, encompassing every aspect of her life: spiritual devotion, dress, diet, behavior, education, and, of course, self-identity. In Islamic terms, it was the beginning of the principle of *Tauheed* – oneness, unity, the interconnectedness, and interdependence of all life. This was a new intellectual concept for Black people in America. It is important to note that even if one did not go to church or practice Christianity, the perception of reality espoused in Christian doctrine dominated American society, particularly Black people who were intellectually vulnerable.

This new worldview, introduced by W. D. Fard Muhammad and embraced by her husband, Elijah Muhammad, convinced Clara and those who followed her husband that they could do for themselves. They could build a world of their own, reflecting their unique cultural and intellectual capabilities devoid of oppressive Caucasian influence or imitation. Clara embraced this new thinking and became the mother of a new Black woman and a new people.

Mother Principle

For women like Clara, *Mother* is natural, authentic, and more than biology. *Mother* is a principle.[4] From enslavement through the Great Migration of the 1920s, the *Mother Principle* anchored Black people in America. Within a decade, city life's complex social, cultural, and nefarious conditions began to dismember the mother's influence on the then-called "colored people". That dismemberment was accelerated in the late 1960s and beyond until the *mother's voice* (the influence of the Mother principle) could barely be heard among a people seeking freedom. It was supplanted by a popular culture that did not originate from Black people, yet most sought to imitate.

Clara Muhammad developed an intuitive understanding of the *Mother Principle*.[5] Surrounded by the natural creation in Georgia, she observed it in the vegetation, animal life, the soil, and plants she loved. *The Mother Principle* was exemplified in her female biology but is greater than the human female; it permeates the entire physical creation. In the natural world, it is the origin of every form of regeneration. In the human world, *The Mother Principle* conceives, nourishes and births, but also educates and elevates its offspring's moral, spiritual, and intellectual life. A woman does not have to conceive biological children to be a mother; *Mother* is in her *fitra*[6], that is, in her inherent nature or pattern designed by The Creator for human beings. *Mother* is the first teacher, and the *Mother Principle* rebirths life in a regenerative, but always evolving cycle that matures the larger society.

Clara Muhammad was the *Mother Principle* in action. *Mother Leadership*[7] comes from the *Mother Principle* and inspires action guided by compelling insight, commonly called *Mother Wit* or *Female Intuition*. Clara Muhammad was a woman of extraordinary *Mother Leadership*. Conventional leadership concepts suggest it is a product of interpersonal interaction and not inherent traits that reside in the individual. However, *Mother Leadership* is an innate dynamic force that G-D created and G-D inspired in women. It nurtures, instructs, and leads to ensure the survival and progress of its progeny – human society. Harriet Tubman exerted *Mother Leadership* when she took charge of freeing her people from slavery. Clara demonstrated *Mother Leadership* when she stood up to the police and refused to sacrifice her children to a public school she knew would harm them.

In contrast to *feminism* and *womanism*, *Mother Leadership* is not an *ism* crafted to respond to grievances, mistreatment, or exclusion, whether perceived or real. It is not in competition with men or maleness, but functions within its own natural space. Therefore, it keeps human life, male or female, in balance and fosters justice; it is righteous, progressive, not subordinate or disruptive. *Mother Leadership* has a unique voice that comes from a spiritual place that speaks with authority. Even a little girl can talk about the voice of her mother when she rebuffs wrong or demands right. It is what makes the feminine powerful. Deloris Williams in 1993, wrote of *"the uncanny resilience of the mothering/nurturing, caring/enduring and resistance capacities...of the Black woman [that inspires] a spirit of hope...."*[8] This writer contends that Williams's description essentially refers to Mother Leadership.

The concept is enshrined in The Qur'anic Arabic word for mother - *UMM* - which means "origin", "source", "foundation". From the root *'amma'* which means "to repair", "lead the way", and "lead by one's example". From this root word comes *Ummi* – my mother; Imam – leader; and *Ummah* – community. Each term represents the natural progression of human development. The life of Clara Muhammad that unfolds in this biography reveals that she exemplifies each progression – 1) helpmate to her husband, 2) mother to her biological children, and 3) leader of women and cultivator of education to the larger society/ community.

Black women historically come from a *Mother Orientation*

consistent with nature (the natural world) and the best of ancient African and human cultural traditions. *Mother* was wise, respected, and obeyed. She projected a sense of communion and obedience to G-D, a higher power, nature, family, and community. Such thinking created unity and gave direction to children – that they must be morally upright, respect the natural world, strive for excellence, and reach back to help others in the race or ethnic group. Clara's sense of *Mother Leadership* was the norm in her family. She witnessed it in her community.

The old Negro spiritual, "Sometimes I Feel Like a Motherless Child…a long, long way from home"[9], signifies the depth of pain in a people who were stripped of the knowledge of themselves during enslavement then sent out to find their way in an oppressive world. The sentiment in that spiritual is a call for Mother because Mother Leadership heals, nourishes, and provides strength and resoluteness. It was the best and only tool that Clara, a poor Black formally uneducated female, had to work with in an oppressive American environment. It was pure, spiritually motivated, and G-D directed. *Mother Leadership* is an *inheritance, a birthright for women*. To the best of her ability, Clara Muhammed used it to support a people's movement towards their human destiny through all of her evolutions. Even as her last name changed - Evans, Poole, Karriem, and Muhammad – her strength and determination remained consistent. Her influence on women, education, and Muslim leaders spans five generations of Muslims within the largest identifiable community in the United States of America. To that community, she is Mother Clara.

When Clara moved to Chicago with a six-month-old baby and six other children, she embarked on the long final phase of her life. The police incursion in Detroit had successfully closed the Allah Temple of Islam and the University of Islam school. Clara had escaped jail because she was at home with her newborn baby (Wallace) and six other children when the police stormed the Temple/School. Her fellow Muslim men and women had been jailed and shaken but not deterred. They believed that establishing *The Lost Found Nation of Islam in the Wilderness of North American* required a battle, and Allah would support them in their struggles.

External challenges were expected; internal dissent was not. The threats against her husband's life by rival dissidents was real, and that possibility changed Clara. Added to that menace were the verbal and physical altercations she continued to have with her sister-in-law Grace, the wife of Kallatt, who lived on the first floor of the rental house both families shared in Detroit. Clara became no-nonsense, driven, and extraordinarily protective of her children. She would fight. Her laser focus was to protect her husband, her children and survive. She was a mother with a mission from G-D and committed to all that implied.

Negative media reports followed Elijah and Clara to Chicago. To bring people to the Allah Temple of Islam and counter the negative articles in the *Chicago Defender* newspaper, Elijah started a weekly tabloid called *The Final Call to Islam.* There is no credible evidence to confirm the extent of Clara's involvement in the production of *The Final Call to Islam* or the articles written by her husband. It is clear, however, that he always relied heavily on her judgment, particularly in the early period of the Nation of Islam, as her formal education exceeded his. The first edition of the paper (Vol. 1 No. 1), dated August 11, 1934, featured a picture of W.D. Fard Muhammad in the upper left-hand corner and described as "Prophet" with Clara's husband Elijah in front of 84 men of the Fruit of Islam (FOI). The second edition (Vol. 1 No. 2) is dated August 19, 1934, and edition Vol. 1 No. 3 is the last edition known to have been printed.

Clara was devoted to her family but also to "the Saviour," W.D. Fard Muhammad, to whom she had made promises. She vowed to see those promises through. In the *Lessons of Supreme Wisdom* given to her and her husband, and taught in the male (FOI) and female (MGT) Classes, the subject of one's word was addressed:

Question: "Have you not learned that your word should be Bond regardless of whom or what?"
Answer: "Yes. My word is bond, and bond is life, and I will give my life before my word shall fail."[10]

That commitment, layered over the integrity that already formed the core of her character, made Clara Muhammad rock-solid.

In her early development, as Clara Evans Poole, she was motivated to provide, protect and educate her family because her husband, Elijah Poole, was unable to do so. Elijah could not or would not lead his family due to external forces of the consequences of racism, economic deprivation, depression, and alcoholism. When he was able to reclaim the leadership of his family, he continued to face problems that made it difficult to tend to his family. For seven years, he was evading adversaries opposed to his leadership of the new manifestation of Islam in America – *the Lost Found Nation of Islam.* Although he had been designated leader by the founder, W. D. Fard Muhammad, in 1933, members who believed he was unqualified rebelled and sought to kill him, including his younger brother Kallatt. Elijah was forced to seek refuge by moving between three cities – Chicago, Milwaukee, and Washington, D.C. – not only to save his life, but also to establish Allah Temple(s) of Islam.

After two years on the move, he spend the following five years apart from Clara and their children. He was imprisoned for refusing to register for the draft of World War II even though he was older than the legal limit for the draft. His purported "draft evasion" was not the reason but rather it resulted from the contrivance by J. Edgar Hoover and the FBI – whose racist tactics later evolved into the infamous Counter Intelligence Program of the FBI[11] – "to stop the rise of a Black Messiah." Clara had to take charge; she had to lead. Thus, her agency came from the mission, strengthened by her innate connection to her faith in G-D and her commitment to her husband, her children and her community.

CHAPTER 2: A NEW MODEL OF EDUCATION - UNIVERSITY OF ISLAM (1932-1945)

The University of Islam was founded in 1932 by W. D. Fard Muhammad and Elijah Muhammad in Detroit, as recorded in interviews with the early members of the *Lost Found Nation of Islam* by scholar Hatim Abdul Sahib in 1951[12], and in early documents from Chicago[13]. It was a courageous and crude but effective endeavor. The enterprise caught the attention of the Detroit Board of Education primarily because of the diminished funds public schools were receiving due to reduced average daily attendance arising from the absence of Muslim children. It is estimated that at its height 400 students were enrolled at the University of Islam in Detroit. The Detroit Board of Education and its supporters began to work assiduously to cease the University of Islam's operations. When they were successful in their efforts to shut it down, Clara and her family were forced to leave Detroit for Chicago.

By September 1934, Greater Chicago reflected a cornucopia of contradictions. It, too, was a destination of the Great Migration but distinctly differed from the Detroit that the Poole family migrated to in 1923. Like Detroit, Chicago oppressed people of darker skin, and they were also warehoused in an area called the Black Bottom on Chicago's South Side with only a few scattered on the West Side. In Chicago, however, Black people were becoming more enlightened and unified. Although reeling from the ravages of the Great Depression, the city's Black population grew from 40,000 in 1910 to 278,000 by 1940.[14]

When Clara moved to Chicago, it was during the beginning of the school year for Chicago's children. The absence of an avenue to provide education to the Poole children was a monumental concern to Clara. Public education in Chicago and the United States as a whole in the 1930s was a brutal enterprise for those Negro children outside of the protection of Negro teachers. Even under the latter's tutelage, many still suffered from a lack of adequate facilities, textbooks, and opportunities. The student expenditures for Black children were considerably and consistently less compared to the educational funds for white children. Furthermore, pictures in textbooks continued to demean Black people, and the curriculum did not include any mention of African or Negro contributions to the United States or world civilization.

Clara refused to send her children into to an environment where they would likely be emotionally and often physically abused. Emmanuel, the eldest was now 13 years old; Ethel, 12; Lottie, 9; Nathaniel, 8; Herbert, 5; Elijah, Jr., 3; and Wallace six months old. Lottie Rayya Muhammad, Clara's youngest daughter, recalled her feelings at the time:

"After my father met Master Fard Muhammad, we had a decent house in Detroit and food, and we went to our little school. We moved to Chicago because my mother and father did not want us to attend a Caucasian school. Now mind you, when we left Detroit, we left a big mansion house. I mean, we had made it to the top, so to speak. We had a telephone, a radio, everything. We never had either before in our lives, but we had it then. But we gave it all up. My mother gave it all up because she wanted us to have an Islamic education. But when we had to leave Detroit for Chicago, it was back into poverty."[15]

"Coal, wood, no lights, kerosene, washing on the rub board, hanging clothes on the line...I mean, it was just a whole new thing. But none of us felt terrible about it because we were in a school where it was comfortable. We were with our own people, speaking our own language, and we were happy. And my mother was satisfied, my father was satisfied."[16]

But shortly after they arrived in Chicago, local authorities, instigated by the FBI, Negro preachers, and the business establishment, raided the Temple. Before the end of 1934, the Temple and the fledgling University of Islam were shut down. The intellectual needs of seven hungry minds forced Clara to provide just as their hungry stomachs had previously forced her to comb the streets of Detroit to feed their physical bodies. The question was, how could she educate seven children with only an eighth-grade education? A survey of Clara's resources included knowledge from her eighth-grade education in Cordele, Georgia, and experiences from the University of Islam in Detroit. She had the Supreme Wisdom Lessons given by W. D. Fard Muhammad, which described the original people, facts of the Earth, and the Caucasian scheme to oppress Black people. The older children had learned basic knowledge from their previous public school days. Additionally, Clara knew the basics of social skills children need to navigate the harsh world they are a part of. Always looking to the future, she wanted to prepare them not only for the present but also to be leaders in a new world when their schooling was completed.

Clara began to structure a curriculum to educate her children. Her method was to teach all the children what she knew. The older ones would then reinforce her teaching to the younger ones by teaching them what they knew. She decided to teach them in her home in Chicago as she had done in Detroit, where the original school began around her dining table. Clara Muhammad pushed through the darkness of the unknown to engage the intellect of her children.

Ross (2003) wrote of her methods, *"Her own ideas, thoughts and family history as well as Fard's teachings became sentences to be copied, and word groups to be memorized and paragraphs that helped develop penmanship. While textbooks were not available, subjects still included the basics: reading, writing, arithmetic – as well as Temple History on the founding of the Nation of Islam and the myths about the origins of Black people. It was a curriculum that made a point of ignoring world history as we know it and U.S. history as we know it."*[17] Years later, her seventh child, Imam W. Deen Muhammad, added, *"And we learned to think, to have our own thoughts. She'd ask questions and sought our opinions."*[18]

Irrespective of her limitations, Clara Muhammad was developing a new education model. She unified the spiritual and the rational, and constructed a critical philosophy with a positive self-image – the elusive, missing element in Negroes' education since enslavement. Although her efforts were embryonic, as the University of Islam matured, it became the most consequential model of independent education in African-American history.[19] It made education whole, comprehensive, self-directed, and self-affirming. As a results of her visionary efforts, the University of Islam became the vanguard of *all* Afro-centric education models.

Long before professional educators and Arabic teachers were employed in the 1950s, Clara Muhammad knew that Black children needed a positive sense of self. It is assumed she had received some lessons of Black history at her school in Cordele, Georgia. She also had a supportive family and community. She had a love of her mother and father, Mary Lou and Quartus Evans, and her siblings, which is foundational to a healthy sense of self for every child. What *The Lost Found Nation of Islam in the Wilderness of North America* added to her assets was freedom from the oppressive belief that she was less than others in the eyes of G-D. This was the core of the identity problem that lingered in the soul of most Black people.

As The *Lost Found Nation of Islam in the Wilderness of North America* evolved in the following decades, its rhetoric and major publication *Muhammad Speaks* newspaper was founded in 1960 and provided a consistent vision of future greatness. Upon graduation, students either continued their studies elsewhere to advance the Nation of Islam or they were placed in visible service and leadership positions within the organization. This interconnected sphere motivated its members while also providing a visible model of progress for the evolving school and community. The centerpiece of the weekly newspaper was titled PROGRESS, and the visuals, inspired by Elijah Muhammad and visualized by artist Eugene Majied, enabled people to envision their future. The PROGRESS section fostered a "we can do this" attitude. By the 1970s, there would be 52 University of Islam schools throughout the United States and Bermuda.

The school produced what Dr. Carter G. Woodson said was missing in his seminal book *The Mis-Education of the Negro, 1933*[20]. By 1945, Dr. Woodson had more to say on the subject. His critique, among others, was, *"The chief difficulty with the education of the Negro is that it has largely been imitation [of white people] resulting in the enslavement of his mind."*[21] *"...Negro education is a failure, and disastrously so, because in its present predicament the race is especially in need of vision and invention to give humanity something new."*[22] And he agreed that, *"it is high time to develop another sort of leadership with a different educational system."*[23]

Credit is rightly given to Clara's husband for managing such transformations. Yet, a thorough analysis will show that The Teachings provided a comprehensive structure that affected every aspect of the Muslims' life. Education – knowledge of self and kind – was the centerpiece that included the FOI – how to be a man, husband, and father; MGT – how to be a woman, wife, and mother; and the University of Islam – universal education for all. While acknowledging that help came from other supporters of the NOI's educational institutions, Clara Muhammad was the force that kept the school together and facilitated its advancement.

The annual graduation at the University of Islam in Chicago was a special time for Clara Muhammad. She would seldom speak, and when she did, it was only to praise the students and teachers and offer greetings from her husband. She did not speak of herself or her contributions or commitment to the school but would give each student monetary gifts and flowers. The occasion brought her immense pleasure and was a tradition she established and continued until she was physically unable.

Clara loved the school because it was a prism through which she could see the future of Muslim education in America and the world at large. The merit of the philosophical underpinning of the origin of man as presented by W. D. Fard Muhammad deserves debate in contemporary society. However, Muslim education led by the University of Islam in early twentieth-century America was unprecedented. Khalilah Camacho Ali, the wife of Muhammad Ali, recalled those early days when she was a student named Belinda:

"The first school [University of Islam] was at 43rd Street off Cottage Grove. The one I attended was on 53rd and Greenwood, Chicago. We then moved to Woodlawn Avenue, and that was great. I remember when Sister Clara came to the school. We would stand when she came into the room. She did not speak over a whisper; she was humble. I remember she would take her little dark hands and pat and rub them over our heads. I never saw a Black woman carry herself as she did."[24]

Clara Muhammad helped to devise a comprehensive curriculum for the University of Islam which was the first school to teach Arabic language to elementary grade learners from non-Arabic-speaking backgrounds, beginning in the 1950s. She also provided private school status to poor people, engendering their children with pride. Students wore uniforms and began school at three years of age, providing a model for the Federal Head Start program that followed more than a decade later in 1965. The University of Islam was a year-round kindergarten to 12th grade school, with separate classes for boys and girls and a universal worldview consistent with its name.

In his study, *The Black Muslims in America*, Dr. C. Eric Lincoln in 1961 remarked, *"Muslims schools are emphasizing Negro history, Negro achievements and the contributions of Negroes to the world's great cultures and to the development of the American nation. These facts are rarely taught in public schools, and the Muslims may be alone in trying to bring the Negro community to an awareness of racial heritage."*[25]

Students were also taught health and food sciences, particularly the devastating effects of the "soul food" plantation diet and junk food on people's well-being. The physical appearance and health of Muslims were outstanding and undeniable. Muslims were enthusiastic about learning, and the University of Islam became a jewel in the crown of *The Lost Found Nation of Islam in the Wilderness of North America.*

The *Lost Found Nation of Islam* policy was: only the progeny of enslaved Africans could join. No Caucasians, Africans, Latin Americans, Hispanics, Indians or Asians were enrolled. The unique pedagogy was designed exclusively to address the multi-layered consequences of enslavement and racism against the children of enslaved Africans. Critics, particularly those who believed integration was the only path to success, attacked the independent ideology of the school and the Nation of Islam. Over time, scholars and thinkers began to understand the bold independence the Nation of Islam was cultivating. The goal was to empower a people by respecting their ability to think for themselves. For the first time since enslavement, an organization of Blacks in North America had cultivated and promoted independent thought without the influence or permission of Caucasians.

Initially a proponent of integration, W. E. B. DuBois began to be disillusioned about integration as a single operating principle. He saw there was no contradiction in Black people having their quality schools, and stated:

> *"A separate Negro school, where children are treated like human beings, trained by teachers of their race, who know what it means to be Black is infinitely better than making our boys and girls doormats to be spit and trampled upon and lied to by ignorant social climbers, whose sole claim to superiority is the ability to kick "niggers" when they are down."*[26]

If Clara believed G-D had charged her with something when she first met Elijah at the church social in Cordele, Georgia, her vision became clearer when she met W. D. Fard Muhammad.

She witnessed the impact of The Teachings both on the people and, more dramatically, on her husband. Her devotion to G-D with this core understanding crystalized her mission and permitted her to persevere irrespective of the difficulties she encountered. Clara believed she was a woman living under Divine instruction.

As she educated her children, the dissidents escalated their disagreement with Elijah. The major contender was Kallatt Muhammad, Clara's brother-in-law. However, others vehemently disagreed with her husband's decision to deify W. D. Fard Muhammad and declare himself Messenger of Allah. Members were leaving the Temple in great numbers. Official reports are unconfirmed, but several sources suggest the numbers declined from approximately 400 to 25. Clara struggled to navigate dissident threats, police incursions, and economic hardship while raising seven children. Her life became a daily whirlwind as she, Elijah, and a few faithful tried to manage what appeared to be the crumbling of *The Lost Found Nation of Islam in the Wilderness of North America.*

CHAPTER 3: CARRYING THE NATION, PROTECTING THE CHILDREN

How does a woman carry a Nation? The same way she carries a child: one step at a time, one stage at a time. That was what Clara had to do; she took time to balance support for her husband, the mission, education for the children, and the pressing concerns of dissidents.

Clara and her growing family lived in Chicago's Black Bottom at 6116 S. Michigan Avenue, an area for lower- and middle-class Black folks. As always, Clara kept the residence immaculate. She continued to "weave silk from straw," recycling clothes for the children and stretching each meal while always respecting the Muslim dietary laws. Her activities were primarily confined to her home and the small Muslim community. Yet, Clara was aware of the larger world, particularly the travails of the larger Negro community. Such knowledge reinforced The Teachings of the *Lost Found Nation of Islam* and strengthened the notion that Muslims were the bearers of truth to a people deceived and oppressed.

Poor people are stereotyped as lazy and irresponsible. Clara Muhammad and other members of the *Lost Found Nation of Islam* disproved those stereotypes. They were clean, honest, diligent, dependable, and charitable. With some exceptions, such behavior and character were also the norms in the larger Negro community. In spite of their poverty, poor Negroes worked, received less pay than other citizens, and cared for their intact families despite their poverty. Due to their concentration in specific areas, they managed to have representation in Chicago's local government. Although their influence was minimal at first, it paved the way for future activism, referred to as the Civil Rights Era of the 1960s.

Oscar Stanton De Priest was the first Negro, outside of the South to serve in the U.S. House of Representatives (1929 – 1935). He represented the 1st and 2nd Congressional Districts which included part of the downtown sections known as the Loop and part of the South Side. However, politicians, preachers, and middle-class Negroes wanted no part of Clara, Elijah, and their *Lost Found Nation of Islam*. The common people referred to as the lower-class (which most Negroes were) initially had a different opinion.

That difference of opinion was revealed in a pioneering study released in 1945 about Chicago and the Negro condition. *Black Metropolis* by Negro sociologists St. Clair Drake and researcher Horace Clayton was a different kind of study. Some regarded it as *"The best comprehensive description of Black life in an American city ever written."*[27] It described in popular nomenclature the tragedy and triumphs of a people struggling with legally sanctioned poverty, segregation, discrimination, and ignorance. *Black Metropolis* revealed insight into the human condition of an oppressed people. It addressed concerns that had been previously discussed by other thinkers, educators and sociologists, particularly W. E. B. Dubois, Carter G. Woodson, and E. Franklin Frazer. All of those scholars disclosed the increased class and color consciousness experienced during the 1930s and 1940s – in the name of education and upward mobility (bourgeois respectability) as well as the exacerbated tensions and divisions among a people who had been relatively united during and after Reconstruction.

Paradoxically, the conditions described in *Black Metropolis* were the central issues Clara and Elijah were made aware of from Fard's The Teachings. However, the prism from which Clara viewed the world was not the conventional view held by Caucasians and, by extension, middle- and upper-class Negroes., which was if one was to be successful, one must model Caucasians and petition them for acceptance. That was a strategy followed since enslavement and Emancipation, but it had produced few benefits for the masses of Negroes.

The bold call of the *Lost Found Nation of Islam* that Clara embraced frightened people, particularly class-conscious persons who depended on appeasement to Caucasians for their advancement. People literally shook in their shoes when they heard the narrative, especially that the white man was "the Devil". They could not believe that any Negro, especially poor, lower-class Negroes, had the nerve to attack the white man publicly or had any solutions to Negro problems. They thought that only white people had answers to the problems plaguing Blacks in North America and elsewhere.

In some quarters, especially among Black Christian preachers, perverse psychology promoted sympathetic and apologetic demeanor to the Caucasians who had oppressed Blacks with institutional racism for 400 years. They blasted the Muslims for their pronouncements. The intellectual domination of white supremacy was shocking.

In the early days of its establishment, those attracted to the *Lost Found Nation of Islam* needed little convincing to believe that the white man was the devil. The history of his oppression of Black people was indisputable. Those converts were seldom middle- and upper-class, educated folk but lower- and middle-class church people who valued common sense. Some writers[28] [29] concluded that the early Muslims were criminals and misfits; however, this is blatantly false. The Muslim men imprisoned in the formative years of the NOI had been punished for their refusal to register for the World War II draft, to fight for a country that oppressed them, and to fight in wars their religion opposed. They were unjustly incarcerated for three to five years. A corrupting element did exist within the Nation, but appeared only in the mid-1960s after government infiltrators, converts from prison, and those seeking economic and psychological domination of others entered the *Lost Found Nation of Islam*. And even then, this element was only a small minority.

Ethnographic studies of the Pioneers of the Nation

of Islam[30] revealed that approximately 97% were spiritually conscious individuals from G-D-conscious families with a former Christian church affiliation. As a result, they had a consciousness of the promises and prophecies of scriptural texts – primarily the Bible. It was evident to them that numerous Biblical references addressed the condition of the Negro. Yet, preachers schooled in theological seminaries taught from their pulpits that those references represented another people. For the Negro, his justice and heaven were to come *after* he died.

When former Christians became Muslim and embraced The Teachings of the *Lost Found Nation of Islam*, they believed G-D would mete out the promise of retribution to enemies. Clara and the early followers knew previously denied justice and inheritance were indeed destined for Black people in America. Consequently, this call to fulfill the prophesy for freedom, justice, and equality while they were alive appealed to them. This was the intangible power that motivated many early converts to accept the Nation of Islam. This call to prophecy was a standard part of the introductory lecture heard by all who visited the Temple. This appeal of The Teaching is continually overlooked in studies of the Nation of Islam, but it is an underpinning of the growth and achievement of the movement the NOI began.

The notion that the NOI was based on teachings of hate was a calculated response promoted by the powers of the established order in their mass media and other propaganda. Muslims were not taught to hate white people and did not spend much time on such concerns. Clara's husband shifted the original teachings of W D. Fard Muhammad, which had called for beheading devils and bombing them from a "Mother Plane". Instead, Elijah Muhammad focused on developing knowledge of self and doing for self. No significant time was spent on hating white people. Members literally saw them as the devil, the enemy. Because The Teachings revealed how the devil operated, Muslims felt empowered and essentially rendered Caucasians inconsequential, as confirmed as early as 1938 by Beynon in his sociological research.[31] The goal was to make conscious efforts to lessen the Caucasian's impact on their lives. The Biblical reference in Chapter Malachi (My Messenger) verse 4:5-6 was all the ammunition needed to convince new converts: *"I will send you the Prophet Elijah before that great and dreadful day of the Lord comes."*[32] For Clara Muhammad, this was a sign of divine intervention in the affairs of the oppressed, and it strengthened her understanding of her role and mission.

While Clara's attention was on her husband and educating her children, Elijah Muhammad focused on recruiting for Temple of Islam #2. The people of Chicago and the country were anxiously awaiting the Chicago's World's Fair: The Century of Progress Exposition was held from May to November in 1933. Mindful of the devastation of the Great Depression on the country, the Chicago Fair was seen by President Franklin D. Roosevelt as an opportunity to jump-start the economy. He urged the organizers to extend the Fair, which they did, from its original end date of November 1933 to October 1934. Henry Ford, who was responsible for bringing thousands of Southern migrants to the north, had insisted that his company not participate in the Fair. He eventually switched gears, however, after seeing the publicity that rival company, General Motors, generated for its products through its working model of a G.M. assembly line at the Fair.[33]

Clara's interest in the Fair was only to the extent that her husband could find employment related to it. There were few economic opportunities in their neighborhood; employment for Elijah was essential since membership and resources from the Temple were dwindling, and Clara, a mother of seven children, was now homebound and unable to seek outside employment. Nevertheless, her daily work included the Nation of Islam, structuring the University of Islam, and supporting her husband and the community.

Unsurprisingly, the Fair reflected the racial challenges America grappled with in the 1930s and did little to improve the lot of Black Chicagoans. "Not only did the Fair discriminate against Negroes in employment practices, but it also denied them admission and service in numerous restaurants and other concessions. One exhibit, *Darkest Africa* openly mocked them in its displays."[34] The racism displayed at the Chicago World's Fair fit perfectly into the narrative Clara's husband was preaching. *"Why do they love the devil? Answer, because the devil gives them nothing."* The response to the question and answer was, *"Accept your own and do something for yourself."*

Historical records reveal that "Some Negroes boycotted the Fair; others, aware that the Fair was attempting to chart a roadmap to the future, were determined to use the exposition to change the direction America was heading. With the help of the National Association for the Advancement of Colored People (NAACP), a handful of Negro state legislators held up legislation authorizing a continuation of the Fair into 1934 until exposition management agreed to wording in the legislation that forbade racial discrimination on the fairgrounds."[35]

The Nation of Islam Temple #2, located at 5308 S. Wabash Avenue, had been established during Elijah's and Fard's excursions to the area while they lived in Detroit. The conversion rate to the new religion was drastically reduced due to hostility from preachers and the FBI and exacerbated by constant reports in the local newspapers of police incursions and threats of violence against the NOI. People stayed away, which translated into virtually no money for Elijah, his wife, or children. Fortunately, the bonds of the early Muslims were strong, and members came to the aid of Clara and her family. They donated food and pooled their pennies to pay the rent for their house. Viola Karriem, the first secretary to Elijah, was a source of personal support for Clara, but her youngest brother-in-law, Kallatt, formerly known as Jamin, continued to challenge the leadership of Elijah, and the plot to kill Elijah intensified. However, Clara would soon find herself in a new predicament.

CHAPTER 4: SEPARATION – SEVEN YEARS PLUS FIVE

It was not an easy conversation when Clara and Elijah discussed his leaving Chicago for Milwaukee in 1935. Her fears for her husband's life and the enormity of the responsibility of rearing seven children without him were overwhelming. She knew how to appear strong even when her insides were trembling. But all reports suggest that, deep inside, Clara knew her previous challenges had prepared her for this new development. She undoubtedly recalled her decision to defy her parents and marry Elijah even, *"...if all he has is the shirt on his back."*[36] Clara knew she and Elijah were a team, a pair, and she simply had to continue the struggle to help fulfill the mission – the rise of the Black man and woman in America. To do so, Elijah had to be safe, and he had to be free to teach what W. D. Fard Muhammad – the Saviour – had given them. Furthermore, W. D. Fard Muhammad had given Elijah the assignment to go to the Library of Congress in Washington, D.C., and begin to study the 104 books on the Prophet Muhammad (PPBUH), Islam, and world history. But for now, Clara had to get Elijah out of Chicago.

Black folks lived in an area of Milwaukee that was just as depressed as the "Black Bottoms" in Chicago and Detroit. Milwaukee was an industrial town that discriminated against and oppressed its Black minority population in all the ways that were standard in America. Its primary industry was the manufacture of beer founded by English, German, and Dutch settlers. Although less dominant than they had been early in the 20th century, the leaders of the brewery industry in 1935 remained Anheuser-Busch, Pabst, and Schlitz. Negro people neither owned nor operated breweries, and getting or keeping jobs in them often meant having to defend themselves against violent Caucasians. Yet, the promotion and selling of beer was prevalent in their communities. The teachings that Clara Muhammad embraced, however, forbade the consumption of beer, whiskey, wine, and all alcoholic beverages. She was taught it was a part of the *tricknology of the devil*, the white man, to keep her ethnic group economically poor, unhealthy, and blind, deaf, and dumb to the knowledge of themselves.

Owing to their depressed circumstances, many Blacks were attracted to The Teachings. Elijah only spent a short time in Milwaukee but he profoundly impacted its Black community. He established Temple #3 there in 1935 with a small number of devoted followers in the Black area known as Bronzeville. Sultan Muhammad was appointed leader in the area. The dissidents from Detroit, including his brother Kallatt, continued to hunt Elijah, as did the local police and FBI. All members of the Temple were under surveillance. Baker Donahue and his wife, Selma, became Muslims in 1942 and were later renamed Baqir and Tahara Muhammad. They were consistent supporters of Clara and her children during her husband's soon-to-be incarceration. Later, when the public stature of Elijah was elevated in the 1950s and 1960s, a convert in Milwaukee who came to the Nation of Islam in the 1960s said, *"The Honorable Elijah Muhammad was fearless. I saw him at the Milwaukee Auditorium in 1961. He was a little man but powerful; he made big men shake."*[37] Within a few months, Elijah left Milwaukee in 1935 and traveled to Washington, D.C., where he established Temple #4 and began his visits to the Library of Congress.

Meanwhile, Clara was overwhelmed, and the unexpected kept her on edge. She had concerns for her husband's life, but also had seven children to be disciplined, fed, and educated, a dwindling membership of the Temple, angry dissidents, poverty, law enforcement surveillance, and more. She struggled to hold everything together but eventually had to do what most mothers do, she broadened her shoulders. Clara increased her faith and not only functioned but also made progress; her faith kept her from teetering over. Help came from numerous sources, and pressure was relieved from others. Kallatt and Augustus Muhammad, another prominent dissident who started a competing Nation of Islam organization, both died from natural causes in 1935.[38] Financial help came from the humblest of sources. Faithful Muslims like Ephraim Bahar gathered scrap metal on a pushcart, sold it, and gave Clara enough funds to feed her children and pay the rent. Years later, Clara's seventh child, Imam W. Deen Muhammad, reported that his mother said, *"You can say what you want about that man, but he fed me and my children when we were starving."*[39] The Imam honored Ephraim Bahar by naming a Muslim center in Chicago after him.

Prayers and encouragement from the Believers provided additional emotional as days turned into months and months into years. Clara did her part to keep the *Lost Found Nation of Islam* together while Elijah was studying and promoting The Teachings on the East Coast where the Negroes, especially in Washington, D.C., were listening and joining. He successfully established Temple #4 with the help of Benjamin Muhammad and his wife, who coincidentally was also named Clara.

This was an era for both advances and setbacks for Negroes in America. The Harlem riot of 1935[40] was one example of a setback, while the emergence of Duke Ellington marked a significant cultural advance. The Summer Olympics of 1936 in Berlin saw Jessie Owens become the first American to win four gold medals in Track and Field. The election of President Franklin Delano Roosevelt saw the majority of Negroes shift from the Republican party to the Democratic party. Mary McCloud Bethune was named the first Negro woman to receive a presidential appointment as director of the Division of Negro Affairs. Popular wisdom is that Eleanor Roosevelt had much to do with the selection. The radio show "Amos and Andy" continued its popularity, although many in the public were unaware that white actors performed the stereotypical roles. Although commendable efforts were made in academia, the arts, sports, and business, the root issues behind the economic and political oppression Blacks were not being addressed. Most

Negro intellectuals and religious leaders were still obsessed with white acceptance and integrating into a world powered by Caucasians often justifying racial inequities by continued misrepresentation of Biblical scripture.

When she was besieged with the enormity of the tasks confronting her, Clara prayed, read her Qur'an and Bible, and sang spirituals. Her youngest daughter, Lottie Rayya, reported, *"The children would constantly ask her, 'Where is Daddy?' And Mama would respond, 'I don't know.' One day the children asked, 'When is Daddy coming home, Mama?'"*, Lottie Rayya said, *"Clara responded sharply and said, 'I don't know and don't ask me again.'"*[41] Lottie Rayya continued, *"It was hard on her. As little as I was, I would worry about him; I would actually worry. I imagine we all worried about him. I know it was awfully hard on her...I would see her bless the little meal we had with tears running down her cheeks. I would feel so sorry for her because she would be really – she carried a great burden. You will never know how much of a burden she had."*[42] When the oldest living sons were interviewed, they each commented how strong their mother was and said that they never saw her cry.

The children were growing seemingly too fast, and although Clara kept a tight rein on them, they needed to socialize, have friends and enjoy the company of other children. That proved difficult, but Clara had strict rules for her children. The major ones numbered three:

1. Do not spend the night in other people's homes.
2. Do not eat anywhere but in your home.
3. And to parents, do not leave your children with anyone.

Elijah Muhammad, Jr., the sixth child and fourth son, said, *"My mother was a highly moral lady, decent, clean. She was very careful with her personal business and her husband. She was very strong and loyal to my father, his work, and her family. When we were coming up, I think all of us [siblings] would say the same thing. She guarded herself from any influence of the world. You must remember she was a young woman, 38 or 40, when my father had to leave the home. She was never without one or two of her children* with her. If she went across the street to the store or shopping, she always had one of us with her."[43]

"She tried to make her children the best they could be, that was her main objective, her dream,"[44] Lottie Rayya added "She would constantly tell us, 'You are the children of the Messenger, you must set a good example.'"[45] Elijah, Jr. recalled, "She was not mean, and none of the family thought she was. She was just strict."[46] He laughed and continued, "My mother could make a belt turn a corner. Actually, she could make anything turn a corner: a belt, a stick, an ironing cord. One day I got into something, and she was coming after me. I ran. My mother threw a comb that was in her hair, and I know I went around the corner. Well, that comb turned the corner and hit me!"[47]

Elijah, Jr. reflects on his mother, "Clara Muhammad could put a whipping on you, man! I remember one day she whipped everybody in the house, everybody!! Man, oh, man! She was something! She was no-nonsense, stern with a smile but loving. After everybody got a whipping, she would make us a cake or pie and tell us what good children we were. And she kept it all together! And she was a little bitty thing, and she had all those boys, six of us, and I was the bad one, the sixth child, I got into everything." His voice trails as he gets into his own thoughts. He then said, "I guess she knew something."[48]

Clara Muhammad knew how cruel the world could be to Black people, especially Black males. She knew the life-threatening dangers and intimidation tactics constantly launched against her husband and children. She made a conscious decision to protect their lives by keeping them obedient, safe, and in line. Keeping children in line by corporal punishment was the norm in virtually all communities – Black and white – in 20th-century America and most of the world. Clara's behavior was reminiscent of an African mother's reprimanding hug; she corrected them but held them close; she did not cast them out. Clara was determined that her children survive and thrive, and as a result of her actions, they did.

Lottie Rayya remembered when her mother could have been beaten or killed. *"I was there when the truant officer and policeman and FBI used to come to the house. My mother told us, 'I don't care if you don't learn nothing, as long as you know Islam. I don't care if you don't learn nothing else.' She stood there; I watched her. She was a small woman but very stately looking. And she held her ground. She was gripping her fist; she was very upset. She was nervous, trembling, and I hated to see them bother her like that. My mother was constantly harassed by the FBI. She was always in trouble with them because her husband was the Honorable Elijah Muhammad. They were constantly picking and knocking on the door all the time. We knew them when we saw them coming. We would say, 'Ok! Here comes the FBI again.' So she was really fed up with all of them."*[49]

Clara Muhammad would not put her children in public school because the other Muslim mothers would have done the same. Her youngest daughter recalled, *"Sometimes I really wanted to go to learn something because half the time I would know more than the teacher, and I wasn't learning what I really wanted to know. But she had to make that sacrifice because my father told her if she took us out of the Muslim school, the other parents would take their children out, and we would not have a school today. So we had to be sacrificed. But that policeman and truant officer never came back; I don't know why."*[50]

Lottie Rayya Muhammad shares her mother's efforts to ensure their education, *"When we moved to Chicago from Detroit, my mother started the school again around her table. A sister would come in and teach us if my mother couldn't, but my mother made sure we continued our lessons. She called the school work lessons. She would not let us go without getting some type of lessons until the school got re-established. We would meet from home to home for everything because we did not have a Temple [Masjid]. The Temple #2 that was established by W. D. Fard Muhammad and Elijah Muhammad was shut down by the FBI and local police, and all Muslim men, excluding the extreme elderly, were imprisoned. Eventually, the sisters worked together with her, and we got a new place, a hall, and the school started again."*[51]

When the school did restart, it was quite humble, barely existing. But Clara carried the vision of what it would become and shared it with the men and women of the movement. The women of MGT worked tirelessly to ensure that their children were taught in a school that supported their new Muslim identity. The men of the FOI who avoided imprisonment put in great effort to ensure they had a facility. All of the children of the early Muslims made enormous sacrifices for the establishment of the *Lost Found Nation of Islam*, especially the children of Clara and Elijah Muhammad. They were home-schooled, and it was incredibly challenging. When Clara could not teach them, Viola Kareem and other women in the Nation filled in. It was a formidable task, but Clara refused to put her children in schools that demeaned their Black skin and religious beliefs. When the new facility for the Temple and school were purchased, Clara's children had decided they were too old to attend. Only the two youngest children, Wallace and Akbar, attended the new University of Islam.

Lottie Rayya recalled, *"By the time they got the hall, and the school started again, I was ready to take another step in another direction. I just got tired of going around in circles. They didn't graduate you in those days. I used to ask, 'When do you pass, when do you graduate?' They said, 'Ooh well, you know Islam is like a circle, you just go round and round and round!' So I really got tired of going around in circles and decided to take myself out. I was over 18, and I could do that. My mother didn't object; she needed me to help her around the house, and I continued to learn and work in the community."*[52]

Lottie Rayya's decision to leave school and help her mother in the home was an important one. A few years prior, Clara's eldest daughter, Ethel, also made an important decision about her future. Clara's children's entire lives were in service to the *Lost Found Nation of Islam*. Ethel and Lottie Rayya's obligation began when they were eight and five years old, respectively. They were very close, and the hardships they encountered were obvious, but the rewards appeared slight or nonexistent in their young minds. They felt sacrificed and became restless in the fold of the community. Young Muslim women, in particular, faced considerable challenges in the early days of Al-Islam in America, and Clara's girls were no exception. Their long skirts and covered hair drew ridicule and harassment from numerous quarters. They also lacked the recreational and cultural venues other youngsters had. The University of Islam in 1940 was more of a concept than reality. Clara was stern in insisting that her children adhere to all rules and regulations so her two older daughters had to be examples.

From the children's perspective, it was a paradox. They loved their parents and the *Lost Found Nation of Islam*. However, their lives consisted of a mother stretched to the bone and an absent father who dissidents were constantly trying to kill. Seclusion, surveillance and law enforcement intrusions, and severe financial hardship were commonplace. They received homeschooling from dedicated Muslims short on skills. It is reasonable to conclude they felt overwhelmed and vulnerable, and they sought relief outside their house and Temple as Clara struggled to hold her family together. Ethel decided to marry a Christian. Her father, between fleeing from dissidents, found time to expel her from the *Lost Found Nation of Islam* to the objections of Clara and protests from her younger sister, Lottie Rayya. When neither girl relented, Elijah held fast and put both of Clara's daughters out of the community.

Ethel's only son, Hasan Sharif, recalls, *"My grandmother [Clara] was very hurt at Grandfather's decision, and she missed her daughters. Grandfather didn't come out openly and say things, but he missed them too. My mother had three children in her first marriage, and when I was an infant in my mother's arms, she later told me that she was trying to get back in good graces with her family because of the threats on her father's life. And he wanted all of his family with him. My mother and Aunt Lottie Rayya were young and started to rebel about certain things. One needs to understand that with the Honorable Elijah Muhammad, it was his way or the highway. The Nation of Islam was strict.*"[53] Clara fought for her daughters' readmittance. Lottie Rayya was permitted back into the Nation, but Ethel's circumstance was more complicated.

During the seven years that her husband was evading dissidents and law enforcement, Clara was determined that the *Lost Found Nation of Islam* survive. Elijah would appear unexpectedly at the front door, startling his wife and children. Sometimes he would be dressed as a railroad worker, other times in an obvious disguise. His mother, Mariah, constantly worried about his safety. Although he was evading dissidents and law enforcement trying to arrest him for alleged sedition, he and Clara always managed to communicate. It is believed there was always a Muslim brother, a committed FOI in various cities, who would make enormous sacrifices to get information to Clara about her husband. Irrespective of the hardship or long periods of absence, Clara and Elijah would eventually reconnect. They conceived their last child in 1938, and Akbar was born in 1939.

CHAPTER 5: SAVING ELIJAH

When her last child, Akbar, was three years old, Clara received news that her husband had been arrested in Washington, D.C., on Friday, May 8th, 1942. She undoubtedly envisioned the scenario numerous times, but now the probability was a reality. She did not know where he was until the following Saturday evening, when Benjamin X Mitchell arrived at her door. He had driven to Chicago from Washington, D.C., as Elijah had asked him to tell Clara of his arrest.[54] The FBI also confirmed the arrest to her. Elijah had been arrested at 1306 Girad Street, N.W., and was in a Washington, D.C. jail with bail set at $5,000, an enormous sum in 1942. He was charged with violations of the Selective Service Act of 1940 by failure to register for the draft even though he was 45 years old and therefore too old to be drafted.

Approximately fifty Muslims demonstrated at the jail to protest the arrest. Benjamin X Mitchell wrote in his memoir, *The Early Days of Islam in Washington, D.C.*: *"Early one morning, two Muslim brothers from Temple #2 (Chicago) and Temple #3 (Milwaukee) came to see about Mr. Evans, [Elijah Muhammad] Minister Willie Muhammad (Elijah's Brother), and Minister Sultan Muhammad from Milwaukee. I related to them what had happened These two men looked so clean and dignified and seemed to be noticed by everyone that passed by them. They wanted to go down to the FBI office. Before I took them...they asked me to take them by the U.S. Supreme Court. When we arrived, they stood in front looking at the statues of nine men engraved on the front of the building... I was standing a distance from them, admiring the way the people were attracted by these brothers. They really did look dignified and impressive...they decided to walk to the FBI office. They went in and inquire[d] about the Honorable Elijah Muhammad's arrest. The officers began to question these two men. The questioning finally ended in their arrest. They were eventually sent back to their hometown for trial and sentencing.*"[55] Those two men were also charged with draft evasion.

Amid the tragic news, Clara had to balance multiple tasks. She was consoling the wives and families of the men arrested, protecting the fledging *Lost Found Nation of Islam,* addressing the sudden passing of her father-in-law, Elijah's father, Wali Muhammad (William Poole); and tending to her children.

Lottie Rayya reported, *"As soon as we knew my father was arrested, my mother said right away she would have to protect all the Nation's work for it to continue after he was released from prison. She put all the papers in a box, went to the basement, and made a center in the coal bin. She put the box in and covered it with coal."*[56] Her daughter said Clara's thoughts were, if the Nation were destroyed during the war, the community would not know where to begin; they would need those papers to rebuild. Approximately 70 years later (2010), a trove of original documents, purported to number 1,000, were found in an attic in Detroit.[57] The documents were verified as original documents by the families of Burnsteen and John Mohammed, and other early pioneers. To the astonishment of the Muslim community, the artifacts were put up for auction to the highest bidder in 2017. Before the sale, ownership was contested, and items were withdrawn. However, one of Elijah Muhammad's custom-designed fezzes and a star and crescent diamond and gold ring were sold.[58]

J. Edgar Hoover and the FBI sought to thwart all movements that inspired Negro empowerment, including the Brotherhood for Liberty[59] and the Peace Movement of Ethiopia.[60] The national police agency's singular focus on Elijah Muhammad and the Nation of Islam was brutal and unethical. Later reshaped in the 1950s as COINTELPRO (Counterintelligence Program) – to stop what Hoover called "a rise of the Black Messiah", J. Edgar Hoover's crusade to follow up the prosecution of Marcus Garvey with a victory over Elijah

Muhammad. The FBI accomplished its goal only temporarily; the U.S. government could not stop the rise of Al-Islam in America.

Claude Andrew Clegg III, a historian and biographer of Elijah Muhammad, posits, *"Anticipating an organized attempt by the Muslims both to come to Muhammad's aid and to violate the selective service law, the FBI used his arrest as a pretext for conducting a multi-state assault on the Temple People."*[61] And that is what they did. Scores of Muslim men were arrested, and families were broken up. Benjamin X Mitchell, the Washington, D.C. resident who housed Clara's husband, cited the names of many of the imprisoned men in his memoir. [62] Benjamin X was later arrested and served four years in prison for failing to register for the draft.

The faithful came from far and near to the aid of Clara's husband. They demonstrated in front of the Washington, D.C. police station, kept vigil, and helped Clara raise money. The early Muslims had limited financial resources, yet they pooled together what they had. After approximately two-and-a-half months, Clara came to the jail dressed in her long white MGT uniform – with $5,000 to claim her husband. He was released on bond on July 23, 1942. Lottie Rayya Muhammad says her mother enjoyed the fact that the officers had to count $5,000 in coins and dollar bills. Benjamin X Mitchell, who was present, confirmed the event. He said, *"Sister Clara, wife of the Messenger, arrived in Washington, D.C., dressed in a long white robe. She carried a white bag containing the money in pennies, nickels, dimes, quarters, and dollars that was raised by his poor followers."*[63] She delivered the money in a white drawstring bag taken from the suitcase she carried. Lottie Rayya reported, *"My mother said she just stood there and looked at them while they counted all that money."*[64]

Advised to leave the city immediately after Elijah's bail hearing, Clara got Elijah out of Washington, D.C., and returned to Chicago. When Elijah did not show for the next scheduled court date, the FBI issued a warrant for his arrest. It was a Sunday morning when the FBI came. They practically banged down the door, reported Lottie Rayya: *"They were very rough with my mother. They demanded to know where my father was. My mother was always honest. If she said something, you could bet on her keeping her word; her word was bond. If we did not do what she said, she would punish us with no dinner or being required to fast for three days. It may seem harsh now, but that was what it was. I recall once, I did not sweep the floor properly, so I had to fast for three days. Early the next morning, I was so hungry I asked her for some milk. I felt sometimes she wanted to change her mind, but she wouldn't. She was determined that we be obedient and that she keep her word."*[65]

However, when the FBI questioned her, Clara tried to protect her husband by lying. Lottie Rayya recalls, *"The only time I heard her tell a lie was when the FBI asked, where is your husband? She said she did not know, but he was really upstairs in the bedroom. They had a search warrant."*[66] Elijah was apprehended in Chicago at his home. The reports that he had been found rolled up in a carpet under the bed was a dramatic fabrication by the FBI for public consumption, said his family and Elijah Muhammad, Jr.[67]

That day, there was some intrigue among the three females in the house led by Clara. Her husband's Qur'an, given to him by W. D. Fard Muhammad, was on the bed, and they had to get it so the FBI wouldn't confiscate it. Lottie Rayya said, *"My father worshipped his Qur'an and did not ever want to be without it. The three went into the room while the FBI was conferring among themselves and removing items. My mother sat on the bed. She got The Qur'an and put it behind her back. I stood there as a distraction, and Sister Pearl, who stayed with us, was handed The Qur'an by my mother. She put it under her bathrobe and walked out of the room. With the important papers in the coal bin and [Elijah's] Qur'an from W. D. Fard Muhammad secured, Clara Muhammad had her own underground railroad."*[68]

Clara managed the affairs of the small community while her husband was incarcerated, but it was difficult. The authorities constantly harassed her and other parents for not putting their children back in public school. All the Muslim schools were shut down, and all the fathers of draft age had been arrested. The few men left were old. All responsibilities were left to the sisters, and Clara Muhammad was in charge of it all.

Scores of Muslim men from Detroit, Chicago, Milwaukee, and Washington, D.C., (Temples #1, 2, 3, and 4) were imprisoned for failing to register for the draft under the Selective Service Act. Various reports suggest the highest number was 300 men. Some had volunteered to go to jail to follow the example of their leader. The *Lost Found Nation of Islam in the Wilderness of North America* was ravaged by its men, and Clara Muhammad was left to stop it from complete collapse.

The granddaughter of Selma, Louise Allan McKinnie, reported, *"With the exception of a 60-year-old named Brother Ben, all the Muslim men were taken from the community in Milwaukee and jailed from 1942 to 1945. As did Clara in Chicago, the women in Milwaukee led by Sister Selma (Tahara) kept the Temple going by meeting in the living room of their homes. There were only 11 or 12 Muslim women who met; all the men were sent to prison. Irrespective of the hardship, Sister Selma (Tahara) dutifully collected and sent money every Sunday [hand-delivered] to Clara Muhammad. Grandma was in charge; she was the Minister. She made sure that every Sunday, whenever they got any kind of money, a stipend was sent to Chicago for Sister Clara Muhammad to feed the family or to go up to Milan, Michigan, to see her husband, or whatever was necessary. Even if we at the house needed something, it was lacking because she sent it [the money] to Chicago."* [69]

Clara had to brace herself for what was about to happen. Her husband and her eldest son, Emmanuel, were sentenced to the Federal Correctional Institute at Milan, Michigan, for one to five years for draft evasion on December 18, 1942. Approximately three hundred Muslim men also received similar sentences from Temples in eastern cities from 1942 to 1946. Clara's family believed that in an odd way, she found relief in the fact that she at least knew where her husband was. Her worries about him being killed eased, although she knew that he was still in a hostile environment. She knew he would be housed and fed, and that she could see him during family visiting time. As a mother, she feared more for her son Emmanuel's mental health.

After his release, the family knew Clara had a special mother-son relationship with Emmanuel. It deeply saddened her that he was imprisoned. He was her first child, the man of the house in his father's absence. He had protected his mother and family, providing food and security, but now he was imprisoned. To say he was her favorite son would be inaccurate, but Clara had an exceptional empathy towards him. Emmanuel's daughter, Ruqaiyah Muhammad-Farrar, said, *"Grandmother had a tender place in her heart for my father."*[70]

With her designation as Supreme Secretary of *The Lost Found Nation of Islam in the Wilderness of North America*, Clara typed the English translation of The Qur'an. She brought the pages to Elijah when she next visited him and her son. When she could not visit, she sent them in the mail. She later got Viola Karriem and other MGT women to assist her. It is reported that the entire English translation of The Qur'an was typed and given to Elijah Muhammad while incarcerated. Confirmed by the father of Darnell Karim, Carl Omar, who went to prison with Clara's husband and slept in the bed next to him, he said, *"He used those pages of The Qur'an in the classes he taught in the prison."*[71] There was no known Qur'an in any prison until Clara Muhammad brought it in. The Federal Correctional Institute at Milan, Michigan is believed to be the first prison to offer Islamic classes, and they were taught by Elijah Muhammad. He would not have been able to do so were it not for Clara Evans Muhammad, who brought The Qur'an into the U.S. prison system in 1942. When the MGT in other cities learned what Clara was doing, they followed her example and typed The Qur'an and sent it to their husbands, fathers, and sons. This is how The Qur'an entered the prison system in America.

The incarceration of Clara's husband and nearly 300 Muslim men did not have the effect on the Negro community that the FBI had planned. Marcus Garvey's tragedy was still in their recent memory; people began to understand that the new Black-oriented organizations were not seditious or communistic, but were struggling for freedom, justice, and equality. Previously repressive tactics like beatings, killings, and lynchings had been used to thwart progress for Negroes. Now this move by law enforcement to use mass imprisonment appeared to be the beginning of a new disruptive method, as members of other Black consciousness groups were also being rounded up and imprisoned in the 1940s. Rather than denouncing such groups, Blacks increasingly began to support their right to organize.

Clara's challenges meanwhile were mounting. In the midst of all that was happening, the passing of Elijah's father meant she was left to comfort her mother-in-law and assist with arrangements. She was completing only the second year of her seven-year separation from her husband. The early Muslims did what they always did; they stuck together, although their numbers were now smaller. It is reported that Clara wrote her husband and son Emmanuel frequently and visited them once a month. None of the letters have been retrieved.

A handsome and disciplined young man named Raymond Sharrieff would drive Clara in his car to the Federal Correctional Institute in Milan, Michigan, to see her husband and son whenever she wanted. The drive was approximately four to five hours, passing routes of the Underground Railroad in Michigan, farmlands, and small towns. Raymond's presence would soon have a more significant impact on her life. He would marry her eldest daughter Ethel and become the Supreme Captain of the Fruit of Islam (FOI) and one of the staunchest guardians of Elijah Muhammad. His sister, Pauline Beyha, would work as the secretary of Temple #2 in Chicago.

Consistent with her promise to W. D. Fard Muhammad, Clara took Wallace, her youngest son, to visit his father. Although designated as *heir apparent*, Wallace was only nine years old and barely knew his father. As a child, Wallace was influenced exclusively by his mother, and he adored her. Clara would also be accompanied by the wife and son of an early steadfast supporter of her husband, Carl Omar, who was also imprisoned. His young son was a childhood friend of Clara's children, especially Wallace. He would grow to be an Arabic scholar and, along with Wallace, a member of the first official graduating class of the University of Islam. His name was Darnell Karim, the son-in-law of Viola Karriem, first secretary to Clara's husband. When interviewed, he said, *"I remember those trips to Milan, Michigan, in the car of Raymond Sharrieff. I sat in the back seat in the middle, Sister Clara was on my right, and my mother Maggie was on the left."*[72] Elijah Jr. said he did not know his father until he was approximately 14 years old. He was, therefore, often jealous when his younger brother Wallace would accompany his mother to the prison. *"I think I was jealous of Wallace for a lot of reasons,"* he continued *"Wallace had a way about him. All the children respected him and left him alone. We knew he was special, but he never acted that way."*[73]

Clara took Wallace to see his father, but Elijah would also encourage Clara to read verses from The Qur'an to his son, particularly Chapter 31 – Luqman – The Wise. The Chapter is of particular significance because it describes a father giving advice to his son about the concept of G-D, the worship of G-D, and what constitutes obedience to G-D. Less than two decades later, Elijah Muhammad would say, *"My job is to clean you [Black people] up. The one to come after me [Wallace] will teach you the religion."*[74]

Elijah Jr. continues: *"My father did not like to see us idle. One day when he returned from prison, Wallace and I had finished our chores and had nothing else to do. He told us, 'Well if you have nothing else to do, go outside and count the blades of grass.' So, we went outside and started counting the grass in the yard."*[75] He shared more about his brother's character, *"Wallace would not kill anything. Once he got mad at me for stomping on an anthill. He said to me, 'suppose a genie – someone three times bigger than you – would step on you?' He had a connection with nature early on. I later heard it in his lectures.*[76]

"He wasn't the type to get involved in things like I did. I was about the worst one; I had to go to juvenile hall two or three times. I was hanging out with bad boys. The last time I had to go to juvenile court, I remember I said I would not do it anymore because I looked at my mother. I saw that I fretted her. I never got sentenced like the other boys who got sentenced to juvenile detention like six or nine months. I fretted her telling the judge what she told him. She did not defend me. The other parents were crying, saying, 'My child is good, he is a good boy and all that.' My mother did not say that. She said to the judge, 'My husband is in Milan, Michigan, in the penitentiary, and we don't teach him these things.' She left it up to the judge. I was never put away. But I saw her fretting, and I decided I would not hurt her like that anymore. I was never put away and was never in any more trouble.[77]

"You know she was a young woman, and her husband was away, and people were trying to hurt him or kill him, and that was on her mind, and she had all of us worrying her and doing things we should not do. I think she was really so disappointed that she did not have her husband. She was keeping up with him, writing letters of what to tell the Muslims. She would say he was away on the road, as they called it. He went to prison for five years, and she ran the Nation from seven to 14 years. She was worrying with eight of us, her personal problems [health], and then the community [Nation] had problem.[78]

"The best advice my mother gave me was, 'Obey your father and obey Allah.' Many times I heard my brother Wallace say he did what his mother and father told him to do. I think about myself, and I did not do that. I did not obey them like I should, and until today, I feel bad about that. My mother was depressed, you could see it. But I never saw a tear roll down her eye. I want the world to know my mother was a very good and kind person. An understanding person that would help anybody. She cared for people. She went to the schools and had the interest of the little girls and boys. She never looked for any praise. If she got any, she would shy away from it; she didn't want to hear it. She was not boastful, or wanted everything *just because she could afford it. She did not want it. She just wanted to be a good person, a wife, and Believer in Allah. That was all my mother wanted and no more."*[79]

PART 4: A NEW BLACK MAN, WOMAN, AND NATION

CHAPTER 6: CHICAGO IN THE 1940S & THE FIRST SAVIOUR'S DAY (1946-1950)

The groundbreaking sociological study *Black Metropolis (1945)* was an in-depth review of the condition of Black residents in Chicago. It created a major intellectual shift by demonstrating that Negroes could analyze and prescribe their own condition without Caucasian influence. An analysis in the American Sociological Review suggested five major points raised in the study that dominated the minds of Negroes: 1) staying alive, 2) having a good time, 3) praising G-D, 4) getting ahead, and 5) advancing the race.[80] The issue of why Negroes could not get ahead and advance the race was omitted from the discourse. Clara Muhammad's husband, Elijah, defined that problem as *the mental oppression of Caucasian superiority and Black inferiority reflected in lack of knowledge of self and kind.*

The formally educated Black population (the aspiring middle-class) and athletes who broke barriers were providing tangible signs of progress through their contributions in academia, the Olympics, and American sports. Yet, there were increased race riots and segregation, which compounded the misery for all, especially the poor and vulnerable, who were looking for another way. The continued efforts by Black politicians and activists to break the scourge of racial oppression received some help when the Supreme Court of the United States declared white-only political parties unconstitutional in Smith v. Allwright, 1944.[81] Discourse by Black intellectuals on economic and cultural discrimination, particularly those in Harlem, which was the pulse of Black existence at the time, was marginal. However, if discussed, scriptural oppression was not a conversation in the public square, not even among preachers and religious leaders. Even Albert Einstein weighed in on the issue of Black oppression, stating, *"Their [American's] sense of equality and human dignity is mainly limited to men of white skins."*[82] Speaking directly to the American public, he said, *"Your ancestors dragged these Black people from their homes by force; and in the white man's quest for wealth and an easy life, they have been ruthlessly suppressed and exploited, degraded into slavery. The modern prejudice against Negroes is the result of the desire to maintain this unworthy condition."*[83]

Christianity maintained its hegemony, and emerging religious alternatives were few and unremarkable. The worship of a Caucasian image as G-D remained strong among Black people. Denouncing this image added to why the message of Clara's husband was so stunning and vehemently despised by Black preachers. The common man was drowning his depression in alcohol and cigarette addiction, societal scourges throughout the country. Reflected in the Academy Award movie of 1946, *The Lost Weekend* portrayed the downward spiral of an alcoholic. The *Lost Found Nation of Islam* prohibited smoking and alcohol, claiming they were "the devil's tools" that devastated the health and communities of Black people. The minimum wage was $.40 an hour, Jackie Robinson married Rachel, and Tupperware was the craze in Middle America.

By January 1946, Clara, now 47 years old, was a changed woman. Since her marriage in 1919, she struggled for survival and the establishment of Islam for a combined 30 years. The comfort of her parent's home in Georgia was both a distant memory and an instant place of repose if she chose to take her mind there. She missed her father, who loved her dearly, and her mother's health was failing. Her siblings stayed in touch; Mamie had married and remained in Cordele, Georgia. She appeared to be closest to her younger sister Rosalie. Her brothers Willie and Carlton (also married) lived in Saint Petersburg, Florida. Willie would be the first sibling to pass away.

Clara remained strong like iron, reinforced by her resolve

to keep her word to W. D. Fard Muhammad. From 1935 to 1946, she worked unceasingly and held the *Lost Found Nation of Islam* together, with the help of the faithful. The women loved her; her children were challenging but mostly obedient and safe. The remaining few men who were not imprisoned respected her and helped her. But Clara's body was weak; she was exhausted and unwell. Clara was appointed as Supreme Secretary by Elijah in 1935 while he was persecuted and later imprisoned; this designation was a formality. Clara did not need the title to do what needed to be done. Her mission was from G-D, not Elijah. Her inspired *Mother Instincts* guided her, and her promise to W.D. Fard Muhammad was a constant motivation for her *Mother Leadership.* Her keen observation and listening skills, developed from childhood, enabled her to assess the condition of the Muslims, her children, and her surroundings with an uncanny exactness. Clara was not selfish, which allowed her sensitivities to extend outward like a radar. Her consciousness was for the greater cause. She was determined to help her husband build a Nation, and she was exceptional at surveying a person or a situation.

When Clara visited her husband in prison, she received instructions from him that she would write down. The small band of the faithful knew when she was visiting and made sure to attend the Temple. Clara would stand in front of the Muslims and deliver the message from her husband. Nathaniel Muhammad confirmed, *"My mother would stand in front of the Temple and read the instructions from my Daddy. She would entertain questions, and anything she could not answer, she would write down and relay it to my Daddy."*[84] Often before Clara received instructions from her husband, she gave him an assessment of the situation at Temple #2 in Chicago. Although the Temples were officially closed, meetings in Muslim homes maintained the Temple numbers as they would in time reopen. The status of the other Temples was relayed to her by her sister-in-law Burnsteen Mohammed, Sally Allah from Detroit, and the Muslim women in Milwaukee and Washington, D.C. When Clara met with the women of Detroit and Milwaukee, she met to exchange information, execute strategy, and plan for the future. The majority of the men had been taken from their families, but the women sustained their communities. They respected Clara and found strength in her. Even the young people could feel it. Khalilah Kamacho-Ali, known then as Belinda, said, *"You could feel her dedication and strength when she talked to you."*[85] Khalilah (Belinda) was privileged to see Clara up close. Her parents were close to the Muhammad family, as her father worked as a security guard for Clara's husband.

The tasks Clara executed with or without the designation Supreme Secretary were numerous, but two endeavors had major significance while Elijah was imprisoned. First, she organized efforts to purchase space for the re-established Temple #2 and the University of Islam at 824 43rd Street, Chicago. Clara had Benjamin X Mitchell oversee the renovation of the newly purchased property. Brother Benjamin and his wife, also named Clara, were dedicated to her and her husband. He had kept Clara informed of her husband's condition in Washington, D.C., while he was evading adversaries and studying at the Library of Congress. His house became the meeting place for Clara and Elijah when she could get away from Chicago. The job for Benjamin X Mitchell and that of the other men was to convert the Dog and Cat Hospital into the new Muslim premises. Benjamin X Mitchell addressed this matter in his memoir, *The Early Days of Al-Islam in Washington, D.C., 1994.*

The second important endeavor was the purchase of 100-plus acres of farmland in White Cloud, Michigan. A devoted follower, Calvin Jardan, named by W. D. Fard Muhammad, was among the men rounded up and jailed for refusing to register for the draft of World War ll. He was imprisoned at Sandstone, Minnesota, and released a year before Clara's husband. She and Elijah designated Calvin Jardan the first manager of the farm in White Cloud. Dolores, the daughter of Calvin Jardan, remembers her father and the farm vividly. She said, *"I visited the farm as a child and remember the cows, chickens, and how beautiful it was."*

A later manager was James Pasha, the first to receive the name Pasha from W. D. Fard Muhammad.

It was remarkable how the early Muslims pooled their meager resources to make these two major purchases. Dolores Jardan became a secretary to Clara's husband in Chicago and recalled how disciplined Clara Muhammad was. In the 1960s, she married Ronald X Stokes, one of the early, who was later murdered by a Los Angeles policeman in an assault on the Muslim Mosque. Clara's husband advised Malcolm X not to retaliate; Malcolm X and others disagreed with this response to the incident.

On August 24, 1946, Elijah and Emmanuel were released from prison. Other Muslim men had been released in a scattered manner a year earlier. Elijah was two months shy of his 50th birthday. Prison life challenged his physical health. He had bronchial asthma but emerged mentally renewed, vibrant, and ready to build *The Lost Found Nation of Islam in the Wilderness of North America.* Clara's visits and frequent writings kept his spirits up, as she frequently reminded him of the enormity of his mission. Her encouragement and reports of the children and dedicated followers gave him hope and visions of a successful future. She was invaluable in maintaining his equilibrium.

Clara was delighted to have her family reunited following his imprisonment. However, nearly a decade of stress had taken a toll on her physical well-being. The presence of her husband in the home relieved much of the burden and softened her somewhat. As Clegg III, 1997 reported, *"Elijah's years of imprisonment and exposure to prison structures afforded him new information and strategies to advance his efforts."*[86] Cultivating farmland and the production of food was a primary objective. Clara and her husband shared a love for the soil, and with the farmland now purchased in White Cloud, Michigan, they would talk about that project until the early morning hours. The children were thrilled and beginning to know their father. Emmanuel was a hero among his siblings. The community of faithful Muslims who held on to the mission were ready to give their lives. The leadership of Elijah was confirmed; his imprisonment elevated him among Muslims and among the Black community who were observing events from a distance. The small community of Muslims knew they could not have survived without Clara Muhammad. It was now time to advance the Nation.

The First Saviour's Day

The homecoming of Elijah on August 24, 1946, was a major event for Clara and the community of Muslims. Although unwell, she worked with Viola Karriem and others to plan the first combined Saviour's Day/Homecoming event for her husband. It was held at the newly acquired Temple property at 824 43rd Street, Chicago. The event generated a surprising overflow crowd of approximately 1,000 people. Imam Darnell Karim was in attendance as a child and reported, *"The place was packed, and there was standing room only. People were in the main hall, the basement, and yard and on the street to hear Elijah Muhammad."*[87]

Subsequent Saviour's Day events were held on February 24th or 26th at the new Temple facility for the next four years. In 1950, more space was needed, and the event was held at Christian Churches, as all preachers were not hostile to Muslims. The popular Reverend Dr. Louis Rawls, Sr., adopted father of Lou Rawls, entertainer, made his Tabernacle Missionary Baptist Church available to the Muslims in 1957. The Saviour's Day celebration had three main parts, and Clara made certain one part was to present the children of the University of Islam. The second part of the program was the address by her husband, Elijah. The third was a presentation on the need for healthy eating and living, delivered by Dr. Blee Hassan, the first herbalist/naturopathic doctor associated with the *Lost Found Nation of Islam*.

By the end of 1946, President Franklin Roosevelt had died, the United Nations was founded, and President Harry Truman declared the end of World War II hostilities. However, the war was not officially over until 1951. After fighting for democracy abroad, Black soldiers came home to a segregated America that exhibited hostility and cruelty in the face of their renewed self-pride and assertiveness. Overall, the social and economic condition of Negro people had not significantly improved since the Depression of 1929. The assaults and denial of human rights intensified race riots, killings, beatings, and segregation laws. The transgressions were so egregious that President Truman initiated President's Committee on Civil Rights in December of 1946. The mandate was to investigate and begin to document civil rights abuses in the United States to protect and strengthen the rights of American citizens. Truman had some sympathy for the Negro cause and, in 1947, was the first president to address the NAACP. Such efforts were perceived as *crumbs for Lazarus* by Clara and her husband. They had another plan for the Negro: *Leave the crumb offerings of the former slave masters, pool your resources, and do for self.*

By 1950, the *Lost Found Nation of Islam* grew in popularity with approximately fifteen Temples throughout the country. It held Saviour's Day in Chicago at the Metropolitan Church at 41st and South Park Avenue (now King Drive). Clara was in attendance with her husband as they witnessed the recitation of The Qur'an by twelve-year-old Darnell Kariem. Professor Jamil Diab, a Palestinian teacher, taught Darnell and Clara's youngest children, Wallace and Akbar, who were students at the University of Islam. Each demonstrated outstanding study of the Arabic language and The Qur'an. When questioned a decade or so later about the three students, Professor Jamil Diab is reported to have said: *"Darnell was the Qari – the excellent reciter; Akbar was the excellent speaker of Arabic, and Wallace was excellent at translation, seeing the meaning inside the words."*[88] On another occasion, when asked who was the *best* student, Professor Jamil Diab replied, *"Wallace. He is sensitive and a thinker, and will be the best help to his father. He sees the answers inside the question and the question inside the answers."*[89]

When interviewed for this biography, Imam Darnell

Kariem said, *"An example of what Professor Jamil Diab was referring to regarding Imam W. Deen Mohammed (Wallace) is how he translated The Qur'an."*[90] Following is one example of Suratul Yusuf (Joseph) 12:2.

"We have sent it down as an Arabic Qur'an so you may learn wisdom."
Abdullah Yusuf Ali Translation

"We have revealed The Qur'an in Qur'anic Arabic so you may practice good sense using your brain.
Imam W. Deen Mohammed Translation

At the Saviour's Day celebration, on behalf of the students of the University of Islam, Darnell Karim called the Adhan and recited from The Qur'an, Chapter 93, Al Duha – The Glorious Morning Light. Wallace and Akbar demonstrated the positions of salat – the formal universal Muslim prayer. It is reported that Clara and Elijah, who were seated on the front row, cried tears of joy. A new generation of Muslims was birthing themselves in 1950.

The activities were also witnessed by a four-year-old named Ibrahim Pasha. He was brought to the event by his grandmother, Malikah Omar, an early convert of W. D. Fard Muhammad. She raised her grandson, who would become a lifelong member of the Nation of Islam. Thirty years later, he would become the first Imam of the Atlanta, Georgia, community as it transitioned from the Nation of Islam Temple to Atlanta Masjid of Al-Islam, supporting the leadership of Clara's son, Wallace (Imam W. Deen Mohammed).

CHAPTER 7: RECONSTRUCTING THE IMAGE OF MAN, WOMAN, AND FAMILY

Structuring the *new Nation* required changing the mind and behaviors of Black men and women. Demeaning stereotypes of Black men and women being cowardly, shuffling, irresponsible, immoral, subservient, ignorant, or angry had to be challenged. But more important, the deep-rooted feelings of inferiority within needed to change. The process for igniting such change began in the unprecedented classes of the Fruit of Islam (FOI) and Muslim Girl Training and General Civilization Classes (MGT&GCC).

Fruit of Islam (FOI)

In the FOI class, Black men were exposed to The Teachings of W. D. Fard Muhammad. The male followers were taught by knowledgeable Black men and learned how to be men, husbands, and fathers. They were also instructed on proper hygiene, managing their money, pursuing a woman in a dignified manner, being sensitive to their wives, producing and working for their dignity and respect, taking care, providing for their children, and other related topics. Many Black men never knew their fathers but had surrogate fathers and brothers in the FOI. The FOI set a high standard for how to be an exemplary Black man. It taught men to build a brotherhood. More than any other institution in the Black experience, the FOI stood Black men up, cleaned them up, and inspired them to take responsibility for their lives and to build a nation of their own.

The instruction went beyond the physical level. The FOI confronted the mental oppression Black men had endured under 400 years of intergenerational white supremacy and Black inferiority. The results were miraculous, inspiring men in the Nation of Islam and those who were not followers. The FOI made a lasting impression on Black men that remains unmatched. Men were clean, clean-cut, ethical, and courteous. They refrained from smoking, drugs, alcohol, cursing, fighting, and extramarital sexual relationships. Men obeyed the law, took care of their children, wives, mothers, and families. They were responsible, their word was bond, and they could be trusted. They protected their people and brought pride to the Black community. Women were "swooning" over the righteous, fine men of the FOI; they had never witnessed a man like him before.

Men were also taught a code of conduct to keep their righteous behavior in check: Muslim men traveled in pairs; they were never to be alone with a female who was not their wife. When they sold their products and the *Muhammad Speaks* newspaper, they were not to enter women's houses unless they had another Muslim brother with them. They were to be cordial and professional but not personal with females. They were never to touch other women. If any Muslim man violated the code of conduct, particularly having sex outside of marriage, he would be expelled from the Nation of Islam.

Malcolm X was an outstanding teacher of men in the FOI and the Temple structure as Minister of New York, Philadelphia, and throughout the country. Other exceptional leaders who exemplified manhood include Elijah Muhammad, Jr., Captain Joseph (Yusuf Shah) of New York, Captain Ali Rashed, Supreme Captain Raymond Sharrieff, and a host of others.

Women's Health, Natural Beauty and Civilized Behavior

The safety, education, health, and beauty of Black women were of primary importance to Clara Muhammad, and her husband agreed with her. Clara religiously followed the teachings of W. D. Fard Muhammad, who established separate classes for females – the MGT&GCC. The model was consistent with The Qur'an, which revealed, *"And the male is not like the female."*[91] Male-female relations and chastity among the unmarried were critical, and punishable if transgressed. There was a conscious effort to counter the negative image of Black women that lived in the subconscious of America as immoral whores and thieves. Wife, mother, and sister were the titles the women lived up to, and Clara Muhammad was the model.

During the early days of founding the *Lost Found Nation of Islam*, Muslim women went door to door collecting donations, handing out pamphlets, and spreading the word of the new faith. They were called *Mission Women*, and although there was an increased respect for them in local neighborhoods, the issue of their safety remained a major concern, as they were vulnerable. Clara's husband decided, and it is supposed that Clara agreed, that Muslim women would no longer put themselves in perilous situations that.

Instructions to the MGT&GCC were specific:
1. Muslim women and girls were to always travel in pairs.
2. They were not to engage in conversation with strange men. And strange men were never to put their hands on them.
3. They were never, ever to be in the street alone after dark/sunset.

With few exceptions, women had a soft, protected place in the Nation of Islam. A review of their status in the broader Black community confirms this assertion. Consistently shortchanged in the larger society, *The Lost Found Nation of Islam in the Wilderness of North America* elevated all Black women. It focused on her complete life – internal and external – regardless of her educational achievement, family status, skin color, or financial circumstances. The Nation felt like home to Black people because it addressed every aspect of one's life. It knew the pathologies Black people suffered from 400 years of dehumanization, and The Teachings given to Elijah Muhammad by W. D. Fard Muhammad sought to address them.

The MGT Classes enabled women to identify their inherent qualities and improve communication and organizational skills. However, the primary focus was always to be the best wife and mother and raise good obedient Muslim children. When asked how her grandmother saw herself, Ruqaiyah Muhammad-Farrar responded, *"Grandmother saw herself as strong, knowledgeable, grateful and humble."* She continued, *"My grandmother had specific guidance for women. She would tell us and them:*

- Be honest, honorable women.
- Don't just sit around with nothing to say.
- If you have something in your mind you want to say, take your time.
- Do not do anything in anger but speak up for yourself. Always have a voice. Never be a yes, yes kind of person.
- Don't ever be a doormat; do not let anyone run over you.
- Make certain before you open your mouth that you are correct, that you speak the truth, and that you never ever do anything shameful to yourself, your family, or to Allah.
- Always seek Allah's guidance first.
- Learn as much as you can.
- Be strong, stay busy, and always strive to better yourself.
- When the sun comes up, you should be up.
- Always clean and dress yourself.
- When noon comes, you should in no way be in your nightclothes.
- Even if you don't feel well, clean and dress yourself, and you will feel better.
- Your house must always be clean and neat.
- Make yourself presentable as if someone was coming to

visit.

- Make sure you take care of your children. Be very careful with them.

Ruqaiyah continues, *"My grandmother would not correct you in front of others. She would always take you to the side. She would give you an opportunity to give your point of view. She would then tell you hers, strongly and directly. She would give you her undivided attention and look you straight in the eyes. When it was all over, you would know you had an encounter with her."*[92]

The MGT&GCC taught civilized behavior, reverence education, eating for health and beauty, love oneself and kindness – especially one's skin color and hair – and live a high moral life and a chaste life if one was single. The social graces of the MGT were distinct. They did not eat on the street and drink out of bottles; they did not cross their legs at the knee; they were not lewd, loud, boisterous, or vulgar, and they were not cozy with men; men were kept at a distance. Bourgeois Negroes were often dismissive of lower-class Negroes and initially perceived Nation of Islam women as lower-class. When they actually met and interacted with them, however, most realized they were mistaken. Class and color consciousness was not an issue for Muslim women, who embraced their fellow Black sisters with respect. That was a mental disorder created by the consequences of enslavement and racism fostered by Caucasians. The Sisterhood of the MGT was to break down artificial walls erected to separate Black people.

The notion that the MGT&GCC only taught women to cook, sew, clean, and take care of their husbands is inaccurate. While Clara and others did teach these skills rigorously, at the core was home management science, a foundational art for the social development of a people. Women and girls were required to know how to cook and manage a home. They had to pass an introductory practicum to prove they could prepare the staples to sustain a home: bean soup, whole wheat bread, and bean pie.

As the *Lost Found Nation of Islam* progressed, particularly beginning in the late 1950s, the larger society began to realize that the MGT&GCC also taught women *"how to act at home and abroad."*[93] This focus was an expansive curriculum focusing on civilized behavior in the public square. A question in the Supreme Wisdom (Lesson No 2, Question 18) asks, *"What is the duty of the civilized? Answer: To teach the uncivilized who are savage, civilization."* The beauty of the Muslim woman began to be redefined with her unique behavior and dress. The focus was not to integrate or imitate an oppressive system but to create a new system where one could live in peace, loving oneself, and being kind.

Clara Muhammad would not emote with an open mouth or with a loud laugh or yell across a room in public. She was not boisterous or rude. Instead, she would smile politely, nod her head or greet sisters with the traditional Muslim greeting. It was a demeanor taught and emulated by countless women in the MGT&GCC as they reached for a more refined, civilized presentation of themselves. Her posture and manner were impeccable; not stiff or artificial, but elegant, regal, and civilized. She did not copy the behavior of Caucasian women. Clara and Muslim women demonstrated that their carriage was rooted in ancient Black people's nobility and high civilization; they were taught their ancient history in MGT&GCC and the University of Islam.

But more importantly, Clara Muhammad and Muslim women reflected the elegance that was innately theirs. In an environment of peace and freedom, they could express what was naturally in their souls. In the privacy of her home or with other women, she would be more relaxed, humorous, but still dignified and refined. Clara was in touch with the best of her human nature, and how Muslim women carried themselves in public *and* private was important. As a link from the past to the present, Clara Muhammad, in her quiet dignity, inspired women to be their best by claiming their own identity. Many Muslim women shared the desire to reach their fullest potential and were simply waiting for the opportunity to do so. The position in the *Lost Found Nation of Islam* put simply was: secure the home and family first.

The Christian eschatology embraced by most Black people espoused that they would have heaven after death. Clara was learning that one could have heaven now. That singular concept cultivated a new religious understanding that the material and spiritual were both essential and a part of worship. Al-Islam historically focused on seeking knowledge, and that acquiring knowledge increased the intellect and the spiritual. That teaching inspired Muslim women to learn Arabic, Spanish, and French. Studying geography and the social graces that reflected high civilization gave them the sense that they were global citizens and *Mothers of Civilization*. This was different from *bourgeois respectability*. The false narrative that the Nation of Islam comprised the dregs of society persists though proven inaccurate. Some members came from the harshest circumstances, but not the majority. A more unbiased analysis is that the *Lost Found Nation of Islam* transformed those from the harshest of circumstances, rendering their original circumstances unrecognizable, and thereby representing an accurate test of its power.

Progressive teachings prevailed even among the early followers who had less formal education because the education they had received from the Nation of Islam was mainly practical. Sisters with unique expertise taught additional classes beyond the regular curriculum. For example, several Muslim women were fluent in Spanish. Therefore, Spanish was taught at every MGT Class, although it was not officially in the MGT curriculum. When more formally educated people came to the Nation in the late 1950s and 1960s, the level of instruction in the MGT&GCC advanced exponentially because of the knowledge and skills they brought with them. Muslims could filter what was beneficial for Black people and what was not from their formal education. Like Clara, most members were G-D-fearing people who had strong moral convictions. They were disturbed about the continuous oppression they were experiencing from

Caucasians because of their skin color.

For Muslim women, tea parties were not just for tea. The social graces of hosting, preparing a table, and making guests comfortable were taught and perfected. Courtesies, patience, and good behavior were taught and promoted. Arguments were abhorred, name-calling unheard of. Civil disagreement and resolution of conflicts were monitored. If intervention was required, Captains and Lieutenants of the MGT were there to assist. There was no breach in the sisterhood; the same for the men. There was a degree of formality that engendered discipline and civilized behavior. Behavior that was too casual represented disrespect or lack of awareness of one's inherent dignity. It was referred to as *slack,* and no Muslim was to be *slack.* Gossip was sinful and destructive. Women saw themselves as queens and carried themselves as such. The goal was righteousness and refinement. The protocol was essential, and produced an environment of order and discipline.

Arguments have been made that Muslim women adopted Victorian practices of femininity because they later wore faux pearls and white gloves. Clara Muhammad indeed wore both. However, Victorian images of femininity and beauty originated in ancient Kemet (Egypt/Nubia/Kush) and were appropriated by virtually every other civilization. Muslim women were simply reclaiming what was originally theirs. For Clara Muhammad and Muslim women of the Nation of Islam, original, natural, and healthy were the operating principles. One's physical appearance was a primary concern, to be an example for the young and, if married, pleasing to oneself and husband. Women were taught how to manage their hair naturally and prepare natural skincare regimens. Clara kept her hair in its natural state; she did not straighten her hair. In her later years, she sometimes wore a short wig due to her illness and loss of hair. Excessive make-up and nail polish were avoided. Women were not to copy the dress or behavior of Caucasian women.

Subsequently, the MGT uniform was a focal point of order and discipline, but also of beauty. It was here that Clara saw major roles for Ethel and Lottie Rayya. The overt emphasis on sexuality in contemporary society as the central attraction of a woman was understood to be demeaning and destructive. That aspect of the woman was relegated to the home and private chamber of husband and wife; it was not meant to be overtly displayed in public spaces. Black women lived with that scourge for decades, and the *Lost Found Nation of Islam* sought to remove it from them. In the 1930s, 1940s, and early 1950s, women had three uniform colors; white, red, and green, with white being the uniform color for Sundays.

Selected by W. D. Fard Muhammad, the colors corresponded with his symbolism of white for purity, red for the Muslim flag, and green, which was the favorite color of Prophet Muhammad, PPBUH. As the Nation evolved, other tones and shades were added. White remained the formal dress uniform; however, beige was added for spring and summer; brown was the official MGT uniform color for fall and winter. Varying shades of red and green, from maroon to lime green, were designated for the Vanguard (the elite, younger, more disciplined core of the MGT). To enable the Vanguard to be more agile as protectors of the MGT, a contest to develop a unique uniform was announced, resulting in the pants-skirts being adopted.

Cleanliness in all things was essential, including a Muslim woman's handbag. Handbags were checked upon entering MGT Class and Temple meetings. They were always to contain a pen and paper and nothing but essentials. The MGT&GCC was a laboratory and a classroom that cultivated leadership skills, sisterhood, and a bond between women that engendered respect, love, and commitment. The classes also stressed physical fitness and weight management, and enabled women to separate their identity from men. The separation of the sexes also gave Muslim women an attractive mystique. Men often inquired, *"What do you women learn in MGT Class?"*

Clara understood that she had a separate identity from her husband. Future actions by him would crystalize that reality.

The issue of a new identity is what strengthened Clara and Muslim women generally. Women in the MGT&GCC, particularly in the 1950s through 1970s, enjoyed the mental space of global citizens, although few left the United States. W. D. Fard Muhammad said in the Supreme Wisdom, *"I can sit on top of the world and tell everyone that the most beautiful Nation is in the wilderness of North America. But do not let me catch any Sister other than herself in regards to living the Life [Islam] and weighing properly."*[94] Clara's husband, Elijah, said, *"I can take the Black woman anywhere, and she will stand at the top of civilization."*[95]

Clara's Guidance to Women

During the 1960s, the second emergence of feminism, prompted by the publication of Betty Friedan's *The Feminine Mystique*, permeated the United States. It was appealing to many women. Birth control, which had been promoted since the early 1914s by Margaret Sanger, gained traction along with her promotion of eugenics – population control for those deemed genetically "undesirable" – which inevitably included Black women. Her original American Birth Control League of 1921 was renamed Planned Parenthood in 1942. Originators of the Feminist Movement wanted to be liberated from any and all authorities they believed governed their lives.

Their original publication, *The Woman Rebel*, specifically mentions G-D and masters. In each instance, their philosophy of liberation was a response to perceived restrictions in the culture fostered by the Judeo/Christian religious traditions they felt stifled their social mobility, especially the role of the traditional wife as homemaker and mother. Their cause rang true on many levels, but it was not the cause of Black women. Yet, as history confirms, many Black women followed the lead of Caucasian women and embraced feminism as Caucasian defined it. The majority of Black women remained G-D conscious and wanted their Black men to have leadership in the society. They preferred to be in the home raising their children, but they had to work outside the home. Some younger women were influenced by the rhetoric, particularly university students and those financially strong. The majority of Muslim women were not influenced.

The language of feminism that evolved in American culture was intertwined with the corporate and entertainment industries. As the Nation of Islam became more influential, it became the target of feminists, especially Black feminists. It appeared that forty-plus years of productively enabling Black men to stand as responsible husbands and fathers became "patriarchy" – a term white feminists taught to Black feminists. Encouraging Black women to cover their bodies, marry, have sex only with their husbands, create a home life, and have babies was defined as "gender oppression."

Prof. Edward E. Curtis IV, in *Black Muslim Religion in the Nation of Islam*, 2006, suggests, *"Muslim women found great comfort in the message of rescue, protection, and respect."*[96] Prof. Bayyinah Jeffries, A *Nation Can Rise No Higher Than Its Women*, 2014, concurs, but notes that the academicians who have written on the Nation of Islam have a divergent opinion. She states explicitly, *"Ula Yvette Taylor challenges the Nation's claims of protection and respect for women, suggesting that this was simply masked, disingenuous and patriarchal sentiment. Paulette Pierce and Brackett Williams agree with Taylor, suggesting that these assertions were a chauvinist helping hand through the double-revolving back doors of racial and economic tyranny."*[97]

For more than half a century, the academy has refused to sufficiently address the most consequential social-religious movement in American history – the Nation of Islam. Yet, within the framework of feminism emerge analyses that are at best as myopic and anachronistic as those deemed scholars pick through the waste of a forty-five-year-old organization. The notion of Caucasian's using the Black intellect to its detriment is what Elijah Muhammad and Dr. Carter G. Woodson passionately preached. Such behavior historically rendered Black people caricatures and imitators rather than leaders and innovators.

Known as a leader of the feminist movement, Gloria Steinem, in a March 19, 2015, interview with Black

Enterprise Magazine, said, *"Black Women Invented the Feminist Movement."* [98] *"I thought they invented the feminist movement; I know we all have different experiences, but I learned feminism disproportionately from Black women,"* she said. Black women appear to misunderstand that their unprecedented efforts as mothers fighting for justice and equality were a model that numerous activists later duplicated, renamed, and appropriated. Black women historically did not call themselves feminists; they fought, in the tradition of mothers, for the family unit, not for their individual upliftment. Their embrace of feminism has drastically changed that historical tradition.

Return to Naturopathy and One Meal a Day

Clara believed in naturopathy and the wisdom of herbology as did most Black people from the South. That knowledge was minimized during the Great Migration and eventually lost to numerous households as the culture and habits of city life prevailed. Naturopathy was perceived in many circles as antiquated, unreliable, and quackish, particularly when the American Medical Association (AMA) began to dominate health and medicine. Their insistence on standards of practice is commendable, but the disparagement of herbology and naturopathic medicine even today resonates as a travesty.

The *Lost Found Nation of Islam* recovered the wisdom of old traditions. Herbs, natural foods, juicing, and the prohibition of pork and pork by-products changed the diet of Black people in America. Many publicly credited the Nation of Islam for this improvement. Although Seventh-day Adventists and Black Hebrews were mindful of their diets, the Muslims of the Lost Found Nation of Islam were most distinctive and impressive in physical appearance. Muslim women were primarily responsible as they were the ones who prepared the meals and watched over the health of their families.

No group in American history, beginning in the 1930s, sought more aggressively to educate the Black community about the harm of eating the wrong foods than Elijah Muhammad and Muslims in the Nation of Islam. Clara's devotion to the regimen was rock-solid. Since she became Muslim, her life included cooking for large numbers of people, and she was consistently faithful to the Muslim eating program. The discipline of Muslims resonated in their appearance, and the one-meal-a-day regimen distinguished the vocal declarations of their practices. Recipes were given to women in the MGT&GCC and memorialized in the books *How To Eat To Live, 1967 and 1972* by Clara's husband, Elijah Muhammad. However, it was more than their diet that made their skin shine. It was a change in mentality and the pride and confidence that they were a new people, favored by G-D, not cursed.

Clara's instructions to the MGT, as given by W. D. Fard Muhammad, addressed the role of woman as the guardian of the health and education of her family. The Muslims' interest in health renewed the popularity of the Jethro Kloss family heirloom, *Back to Eden*, one of the oldest and most treasured books of herbology. Every MGT was required to have it in her kitchen and live by it. Clara taught the original bean soup and bean pie recipes, which distinguished Muslims. Before the *Lost Found Nation of Islam*, the majority of the Black community ate the diet from the days of plantation enslavement; a few followed the eating habits of Caucasians. Later called soul food, they ate pig – every part of it from the tail to the snout – a food prohibited by all religious scriptures. They ate foods fried in pig fat, foods meant to be fed to cattle, and an abundance of sugar and salt. The result was high blood pressure, rheumatism, diabetes, and numerous aches and pains. Health concerns of the Black population were so prevalent that W.D. Fard Muhammad addressed them in the Supreme Wisdom Lessons taught to all MGT and FOI. Those Lessons, given first to Clara and her husband, were foundational guidance for *How To Eat To Live.*

Clara's focus on health, natural beauty, and civilized behavior resonated. The language construction of the *Lost Found Nation of Islam* continued to permeate the cities where Temples were established. The physical presence of Muslim women whisking through communities gave visual confirmation of their new self-esteem and beauty. In the face of the unchanging social conditions that afflicted the common man/woman, the language of the Muslims grew in popularity. This singular movement called the *Lost Found Nation of Islam* created a rippling effect that impacted the consciousness of Black people from all walks of life. *Know yourself*, *do for self* and *pool your resources* had more meaning in the 1950s than the 1930s. Embracing one's self as Black was a monumental shift in consciousness and was foundational for subsequent freedom and justice movements. In the 1980s, entertainer James Brown publicly announced that Elijah Muhammad inspired him to write, *I'm Black, and I'm Proud.* James Baldwin also revealed that *The Fire Next Time* was inspired by his conversations at the dinner table of Elijah Muhammad in 1961-1962.

CHAPTER 8: CULTIVATING HER CHILDREN AS LEADERS

Clara made certain her children were well integrated into *the Lost Found Nation of Islam.* Emmanuel, Nathaniel, Herbert and Elijah, Jr., Ethel, and Lottie Rayya can be credited with collectively cultivating male/female leadership in education, business, and cultural development in the early days of the Nation of Islam. Clara worked diligently to pair the boys with men of the FOI who were generous with their time as mentors. Emmanuel became his father's first security guard, and Herbert maintained the Temple and school property.

Elijah, Jr., was a leader of men and became Captain of the FOI, working with his brother-in-law, Raymond Sharrieff, who would become the Supreme Captain. He was a faithful and diligent protector of his father and the Nation of Islam. Many FOI credit him with evolving them into manhood. Herbert was inclined to business and was engaged in various financial pursuits. He was a negotiator and an inspiration for the business-minded. Nathaniel was a natural teacher and was instrumental in establishing numerous Temples around the country. He would become a Minister of the Nation of Islam. Emmanuel remained Clara's protector. He stayed close to her and had a unique bond with her. His daughter, Ruqaiyah, said he took care of his mother and the gardens she loved.

It was a logical decision of Clara for Ethel and Lottie Rayya to have a more significant role in the structure of the MGT&GCC. Ethel was outstanding in cooking, business management, and dressmaking. Her persona was larger than life, many said. She was well-loved and personable. She would become the Supreme Captain of the MGT&GCC. Lottie Rayya was the National Captain of the MGT&GCC. She traveled with Malcolm X around the country. He would establish new Temples, and Lottie Rayya would establish the MGT&GCC. She would eventually become the Dean of Girls at the University of Islam, Chicago. She was a diligent worker, gregarious and articulate, but more reserved than Ethel. She worked well with the younger girls and was sought out by them for guidance. She was loved. Clara continued to visit various MGT&GCC's around the country to promote women and education.

The decision of Clara and her husband to give more discretion to Ethel and Lottie was a catalyst to the evolving role of Muslim women. After Elijah permitted his daughters to return to the Nation of Islam, Clara and her husband gave them more room to contribute. Ethel divorced her Christian husband with the assistance of her father. He opened his home to her and her three children, and her sister Lottie Rayya lived with their parents at 6116 South Michigan Avenue, Chicago. Ethel was strong, determined, and endeavored to fulfill her driving aspirations as a leader. Hasan, Ethel's son, commented, *"My mother was influenced by Grandmother, but her greatest influence was Grandfather. She was one of those daughters who wanted to get the respect and love and admiration of her father the way a son does. And out of ignorance or whatever, some fathers put all of their focus on their sons and tend to neglect their daughters, and sometimes the daughter is the real treasure. My Grandfather believed there were certain things men did and certain things women did. But my Mom wanted to move past those kinds of barriers."*[99]

Ethel did move past those barriers and became the driving force behind the newly combined Muslim grocery store, restaurant, and bakery established by her father in the late 1940s. She and her new husband, Raymond Sharrieff, initially lived over the store. From 1953 to 1955, the Shabazz Grocery Store, Bakery, and Restaurant were at 3117 South Wentworth, Chicago. The Temple #2 Restaurant and Grocery was at 614-16 E. 71st Street, Chicago, after opening in the late 1950s. Ethel became known for her cooking at the restaurant and larger Saviour's Day events along with Sister Francis, who would become a cook for Clara. Ethel made and sold creative small fruit pies to Muslims and Black businesses in Chicago. Her *Eat Ethel's Pastries* became famous, and the products endeared the Muslims to the larger community. She initiated the MGT Clothing Factory along with Lottie Rayya and other women to advance the uniform for Muslim women. Also, it was Ethel who refined the Muslim bean pie recipe initially made by Clara Muhammad, Mary Al Manza, and Sally Allah in the 1930s. Contrary to the myth that Herbert/ Jabir Muhammad reintroduced the original bean pie, Hasan Sharif said, *"No. Uncle Jabir was eating them, but my mother was making them. She did later teach him how to make the pie, and he became the manager of Your Muslim Bakery."*[100]

Three sons gained international recognition: Herbert/ Jabir, as manager of boxing great Muhammad Ali; Akbar became the first Ph.D. in the Nation of Islam; and the *heir apparent*, Wallace, as Imam W. Deen Mohammed, became a global spiritual leader, philosopher, religious scholar, and head of the largest community of Muslims in America. All of the siblings adored their mother and gave credit to her for their success. They also agreed, *Clara was tough, strict, and would beat the daylights out of them to keep them in line, and that she put them on the right road and kept them there.*

Clara's children stayed in the Nation of Islam, raised good families, and made outstanding contributions to Al-Islam in America. They also unanimously agreed that Wallace was special; their mother gave him special care and confirmed that he would be the new leader after their father. The first grandchild of Clara and Elijah, Ethel's son Hasan, said, *"Our family was not a touchy-feely, kissy, huggy family. The focus was loyalty. It may have had something to do with that old southern influence and old southern kind of discipline my grandparents experienced. We knew they loved us. And my grandmother was loyal, disciplined, and dignified. I mean disciplined in her service to the Honorable Elijah Muhammad's leadership and just an incredibly dignified person."*[101]

That peculiar southern influence he referenced was

characterized by the need for restraint in showing emotions. It was ingrained into the demeanor of formal enslaved people due to the possibility of separation of family members, death by lynching, interruption of family ties through the selling of children, or other forms of violent separation. Hasan continues, *"Also, the structure and discipline of the Nation of Islam was strict... military...left, right, left, right...hut, ho, hut, ho. It was serious times, and there had to be some type of escape valve. So my family, aunts, and uncles all could have had careers as stand-up comedians. All of them were funny, especially Uncle Jr. (Elijah, Jr.), Uncle Wallace, and my mother. Most people don't know, Grandmother Clara had a tremendous sense of humor. It is also important to understand that everybody was trying to get the affection of the Honorable Elijah Muhammad. Everybody from Grandmother on down. Everybody had the mindset that whatever he said, that is what I must do; I hear, and I obey. And if you did what he said, you were in his good graces. You had nothing to worry about. Life was joyful. And everybody did whatever they could above and beyond what he asked them to do to make sure they stayed in his good graces."*[102] The first grandchild continued by sharing that when his grandfather was a child, he was called a prophet. The family of Elijah predicted that he would be a prophet just like Elijah in the Bible. They saw something special in him.

Clara's wisdom to let Ethel and Lottie Rayya assume more responsibility resulted in the 1960s creation of soft pastel colors as the enduring signature of the MGT&GCC uniform. In consultation with their mother and father, they selected beautiful soft pastels to enhance the purity and beauty of Muslim women. Without the embellishments of any ethnic motifs, even African Muslim women presented a new, clean, unadulterated canvas signifying the birth of a new woman and a new people. Being made in a factory owned by Muslims added to the group dignity, beautification, and pride of the Muslim woman.

The introduction of the revolutionary pants-skirt added to the unique originality of the Muslim woman's uniform and elevated their status. It provided an authentic piece of clothing originated by Muslim women. The self-esteem such an accomplishment generated cannot be overestimated. It was tangible proof that a people could determine their own destiny if they would only think for themselves and not copy Caucasians. Lottie Rayya and Ethel, possibly with input from other women, also designed the MGT bar pin and went to a Chicago jeweler to have it produced. The pin became a signature worn by all of the women in the Nation of Islam. The original perception in the larger Black community that Muslim women belonged to an oddball cult that forced them to wear long skirts rapidly changed.

In 1945, the esteemed historian, Dr. Carter G. Woodson was quoted in the *Washington Afro-American*:

"....across from [my] office in the 1500 block of ninth Street, N.W. [Washington, D.C.], a procession of colored Mohammedans [sic] may be seen going to their little frame Temple several times a week." He said, *"At first we laughed at them, but we are not laughing anymore because these Mohammedans [sic] who pray five times a day while bowing in the direction of the Prophet's tomb [sic] in Mecca prove that some colored people are accepting this faith. This shows the failure of the Christian church. Mohammedans recognize only one G-D, Dr. Woodson says, and Mohammed is prophet. Mohammedans have the advantage of being a brotherhood for all races. Colored people are welcomed by the Moslems but turned away by the Christians.* [103]

"An influence for good, the Mohammedans have instilled temperance into the natives of certain parts of Africa... adding that alcohol and social diseases have always followed Christianity. Christians, both Protestants and Catholic, all say that there is no place in Christendom for Black people. Mohammedans require the freedom of slaves. Over the door of the Mohammedan Temple, Dr. Woodson says, they have inscribed under the sign of the cross these words, 'This sign leads to slavery and death.' Under the sign of the crescent emblem of Mohammed, they have inscribed these words, 'This sign means, freedom, justice and equality."[104]

The separation of ethnic groups was as necessary as the separation of the sexes in the *Lost Found Nation of Islam*. No Caucasians, Arabs, Africans, or immigrants of any ethnicity were permitted in the Temples of Islam. The inherent racism each group – including foreign Muslim groups – had for Black people in America was an additional psychological trauma they did not need. Their racism belittled the Black population, intimidated their psyches and negated their intellect, skin color, hair texture, dress, and cultural mannerisms.

As a Muslim, W. D. Fard Muhammad planted authentic Qur'anic seeds in the structure and teachings of the *Lost Found Nation of Islam*. It is understood that he believed they would eventually take root and grow into the proper form of Al-Islam based upon the universal Qur'an. However, he felt in 1931 that Black people needed their self-esteem restored and white supremacy defeated. In order to achieve these goals, Black people had to come out of the mental enslavement of white supremacy and Black inferiority.

Turner (1997) suggests scholars have misunderstood the Nation of Islam, particularly Elijah Muhammad, in suggesting he promoted racial separation. He states, *"Fard knew that there were historic patterns of racial separation in Islam that came to America with Asian, Arab and East European Muslim immigrants and that these patterns would ultimately alienate African-American converts. Therefore, he [W. D. Fard Muhammad] restricted membership to African Americans and discouraged fraternization with immigrant Muslims. This is an important point that needs emphasis – the racial separatist model of African Americans in Islam was initiated not by a Black nationalist but by a non-Black Muslim from the 'old country.'"*[105]

On the surface, it appeared that Clara had a general healthy opinion of herself. Her weight was excellent, she avoided prohibitive foods, and she was disciplined, organized, and completed phenomenal tasks. Yet, the emotional and psychological pain she experienced found a nesting place in her and developed into a stomach ulcer. Its origin was more psychosomatic (spiritual/psychological) than physical, which confirms the cause was anxiety, stress, and feeling overwhelmed with the preponderance of challenges she faced. Although she was a woman of strong faith, it is reasonable also to suggest that Clara may frequently have had doubts about her ability to manage the voluminous challenges that surrounded her. The Solar Plexus, or pit of the stomach, is a place in the body representing one's core. The unfathomable experiences Clara encountered were critical issues that affected the core of her existence. Her first grandchild, Hasan Sharif, reported, *"I remember it was in the 1950s that my grandmother had surgery; they took out over half of her stomach."*[106]

Wallace Goes to Prison

Clara continued to support the development of her son, Wallace. His quiet study of The Qur'an was his most dedicated activity. In August 1959, Malcolm X introduced the twenty-six-year-old at Temple #7 in Harlem, New York.[107] Wallace recited prayers from The Qur'an, including Al Fatiha, translated them, and gave a brief *khutba* (talk/lecture) on Prophets, messengers, the oneness of The Creator, and the oneness of humanity. His talk supported his father, but the context was broader. He did not mention W. D. Fard Muhammad or refer to him as G-D, and never did throughout his life. He was grounding himself in universal Al-Islam consistent with the revelation of The Qur'an. Clara and her husband kept their ears close to what he was teaching and gave him the freedom to develop. Other officials in the Nation of Islam kept their ears and eyes on him with different intentions.

The following year, 1960, the FBI charged Wallace with draft evasion, and Clara's son was imprisoned for refusing to serve in the Korean War. In his seminal, *Pillar of Fire*, 1998, historian and scholar Taylor Branch speaks to the ordeal of Wallace (Imam W. Deen Mohammed). He wrote, *"In the 1950s, when federal prosecutors denied Wallace Muhammad the military draft deferment due legitimate clergy, Chicago lawyers William*

Ming and Chauncey Eskridge arranged for him to serve medical duty as a conscientious objector, but Elijah Muhammad unexpectedly rejected the plea bargain with white law. Much against his will... Wallace dutifully entered Sandstone, where he taught Islam to inmates in the prison laundry room or on nice days in the baseball bleachers. For the first time, he felt responsible for his own thoughts, and although he attracted a large following of Muslim converts, which excited the fears of most prison authorities, the Sandstone warden became so convinced of the salutary efforts on inmate rehabilitation that he invited Wallace to write an article on the Islamic concept of sacrifice for the 1962 Christmas issue of the prison journal."[108]

Wallace not only taught inmates, but he also taught the Nation of Islam via *Muhammad Speaks* newspaper. In 1960, one article in particular, "Impact of Islam on Muslim Women,"[109] addressed the equality of male and female from The Qur'an. His editorial stated: *"Among the Muslims the training of men and women is given equal attention because The Qur'an makes women the equal of men...They excel each other in some respects, yet they are equal in the sight of God."*[110]

During her son's incarceration, Clara kept herself busy visiting numerous University of Islam schools and the women of the MGT&GCC. They received her with great warmth and love. Della Shabazz recalls when she came to Philadelphia in 1960: *"She was just beautiful, just a beautiful woman; so elegant. I have never met anyone so composed. Nothing shocked her, she was a beautiful woman trying to help get the truth for us."* Mrs. Shabazz continued, *"I think about myself. That teaching of the Nation of Islam gave me strength I did not know I had. I was in my teens, high school. My father was a Christian preacher. My mother went with me to the Temple and said if you believe go with it."*[111] In her response to the warmth and generosity of the MGT in Philadelphia, Clara sent them a thank you letter. Clara was a letter writer and enjoyed communicating even with sisters she did not know. If a Sister sent her a letter, in most instances Clara would respond.

Her son's imprisonment caused Clara great pain, but

Wallace assured her he would be all right. So Clara did what mothers do. She prayed for his safety, wrote him, and sent care packages. Upon his release in 1963, Wallace returned as Minister of Temple #12 in Philadelphia and resumed teaching Al-Islam from The Qur'an, attracting considerable followers.

CHAPTER 9: MOTHER OF THE NATION

Expanding The University of Islam

The 1950s saw an explosion of literature, culture, and business development in the larger Black community. It represented a progression of the efforts of extraordinary thinkers and activists who had long pushed towards freedom. Although seldom given credit, the actions of Marcus Garvey and the unprecedented work of Elijah Muhammad were sources of inspiration. *The Lost Found Nation of Islam* inspired the courage to think independently and to build from that independent thought a nation of freedom, justice, and equality for Black people.

The influence of Clara's husband grew as The Teachings reached the ears and psyche of more Black people. Temples of Islam increased from five to approximately twenty by the early 1950s and would number more than 60 by the 1960s. In the larger Black community, change was reflected in the literature, suggesting increased self-analysis and critical thought. Gwendolyn Brooks of Chicago won the Pulitzer Prize for Poetry (1950); Johnson Publishing Company introduced Jet Magazine (1951); Ralph Ellison published *Invisible Man* (1952) and won the National Book Award in 1953 and James Baldwin wrote *Go Tell It on The Mountain (1953)*. The metaphorical griot continued to evolve, connecting the dots of identity, purpose, and people's destiny.

As the community of Muslims continued to grow, so did Clara Evans Muhammad as Mother of the Nation. Hierarchal structures became more pronounced in the organization, and gender separation more distinct. The structures were not offensive to members. They were taught that they helped cultivate discipline and morality. Evidence supports that discipline in the Nation of Islam was commendable, consistent with historical universal Islamic norms, exceeding many contemporary Muslim nations. Discipline provided mutual respect and moral health for the new community of Muslims and astounded the observing public.

The Lost Found Nation of Islam prohibited drinking, smoking, gambling, extramarital sex, lying, stealing, and all moral offenses. Cleanliness inside and out was stressed for the body, home, and other surroundings. It was so important that *The Committee of Cleanliness*[112] was an official part of the Nation. The MGT&GCC and the FOI stressed high moral conduct, cleanliness, and respectable dress. This focus was offered to the Black community as the Nation of Islam's path to racial uplift and respectability. It was believed these practices were the way to bring a people up in the eyes of civilization, absent of class bias. Members who refused to abide by the rules were excommunicated.

For Clara, it began with the understanding that the white man was not G-D and Black people were not cursed. Clara's character was exemplary and modeled by women in the MGT&GCC. Nathaniel Muhammad said of his mother, *"I never met anyone male or female who had a greater sense of cleanliness than my mother."*[113] She consistently displayed moral integrity, cleanliness, punctuality, weight management, healthy eating, charity, alertness, and devotion. She was known for her commitment to her husband and the Cause of Islam. Like all early Muslims, Clara believed W. D. Fard Muhammad was the Saviour for Black people but not G-D. When Clara called on G-D, she called Allah.

Clara evolved from relating to her biological children, the Muslim community, national and international luminaries, and noble causes. She continued to address education, became an avid reader, and was astute in international affairs, spurred by her husband Elijah's world travels and her interaction with guests who came to the mansion. Her daughter Lottie Rayya,asked her mother to have quality teachers to ensure no more Muslim children were sacrificed as she and her siblings were. Clara agreed and worked diligently to pressure her husband to prioritize education. The University of Islam and education in general became her lifelong work and would be lauded as the model for independent education by practitioners, scholars, and city and state officials.

Three consecutive efforts, foundational to the growth of the University of Islam, were initiated in designated cities with growing Muslim populations. The first was Detroit, where Fern Tauheedah Mahmoud was selected to re-establish the University of Islam. She was one of the early professionally trained educators and was the wife of a devoted security guard of Clara's husband. Born in Oklahoma, when interviewed she said she was the cousin of Dr. John Hope Franklin and that her ancestors were never enslaved. She traveled often between Chicago and Detroit and stayed in the home of Clara, receiving direct instructions from her and her husband. She and Clara developed a mother-daughter relationship with deep affection and commitment. Mrs. Mahmoud said, *"Sister Clara was so kind; she sent me MGT uniforms. She said she had so many that she could not wear them all."*[114] Due to the diligent work of Fern Tauheedah Mahmoud, the University of Islam eventually reopened, acquired accreditation from the Detroit Department of Education, and became one of the flagship schools of the *Lost Found Nation of Islam*. The pioneering work of Burnsteen and John Mohammed, and numerous others, laid the foundation. Mrs. Mahmoud eventually returned to Chicago and worked with the University of Islam as long as her health permitted.

The second focus was New York City. Akbar, Clara's youngest son, taught Arabic at Temple #7, where Malcolm X had been the Minister. Another couple inspired by the work of Clara's husband became members of the *Lost Found Nation of Islam* and devoted themselves to the mission of education. The wife, Sister Jessie X, renamed Aahira Nu'mani, founded the school with the assistance of a member named Sister Joyce. Clara visited the school at its Brooklyn location and was impressed with its progress. The University of Islam eventually moved to New York City in Harlem at Temple #7. It became one of the most progressive schools in the country with state-of-the-art facilities. The new building was constructed after the original was firebombed in retaliation for the assassination of Malcolm X. Enrollment was from kindergarten to the twelfth grade.

Chicago was the third city to advance the educational mission of the *Lost Found Nation of Islam.* Several courageous women stepped forward to assist the school, including Sisters Christine Johnson, Debra Fayzah, and Marva Saleema Salaam. However, the work of Beverly Murad was distinguished by her professional expertise and closeness to Clara and her husband. She was the first National Directress of Education selected by Clara's husband. Her visits to virtually every University of Islam in the country provided instructions and inspiration to the efforts and resulted in improved professionalism and quality of the schools. Sister Beverly Murad significantly contributed to the evolution of the University of Islam schools. By 1975, there were approximately 52 schools throughout the United States and one in Bermuda.

Amid ill-equipped segregated schools in America, the University of Islam was an oasis for Muslim and Black children. It gained national attention and accolades from mayors and educators. Clara and Elijah did not consult with Caucasian boards of directors to determine what was needed for Black children in education. They observed the condition of their people and used their intelligence to alleviate the problems with astounding success.

Before and during Brown vs. Board of Education, the Negro integrationists believed Caucasians knew best what Negroes needed. The NAACP, the National Urban League, and other similar organizations followed the direction of their boards of directors regarding all matters related to the advancement of Black people. Each organization had specific goals but did not include financial empowerment, ownership of neighborhoods and businesses, or strengthening Black family life. It remains a prevailing view that these organizations used the legitimate grievances of the Black community to break down barriers that other groups more successfully benefited from. This is evidenced by the fact that after the passage of the 1964 Civil Rights Act, rather than the U.S. Government repair and correct its past crimes against Black people with reparations or restitution of some sort, it passed legislation that opened the gates one year later, allowing other ethnic groups to come to America. On the surface, it appeared that the allowance of peoples of color to enter was an admirable act. However, other ethnic groups were put in line ahead of Black people. Many of these groups were supported with financial help, land, no-interest loans, and a host of other supportive services. A specific example is the Vietnamese. Many groups were even allowed to move into Black neighborhoods to establish businesses causing greater tension and disenfranchisement. The government demonized the call of self-help by Clara's husband, Elijah, and consistently sent in agents and provocateurs to dismantle the Nation of Islam. The position of W. D. Fard Muhammad appeared to be proven: Caucasian America had no intention of being just and fair with Black people.

Brown v. Board of Education did not achieve its goals. Instead, it destroyed the underpinnings of Black schools and eviscerated the impact of Black professionals, teachers, and administrators who, previously, were the pillars for Black youth. Another major factor was that the Black educational experience was always rooted in a spirituality that disintegrated upon integration. Education for Black children has yet to recover, evidenced in *Brown v. Board: Its Impact on Education, and What It Left Undone, 2002.*[115]

Economic Development and Expansion

The acquisition of farmland and the combined grocery store, restaurant, and bakery at 3117 South Wentworth Avenue in Chicago during the late 1940s laid the foundation for generating income and jobs for the *Lost Found Nation of Islam*. In addition to the unprecedented new thinking taught by Clara's husband, the larger society was impacted by Muslim businesses, schools, and the purchase of a new Temple building at 5335 South Greenwood Avenue. The new Muhammad residence at 4847 South Woodlawn Avenue and the emergence of Malcolm X were inspiring and garnered a favorable response from the larger Black community. These monumental achievements, at the time, provided a living model that Black people could produce for themselves. Clara did not work in the bakery/restaurant, but her ideas and influence were present through her daughter Ethel, who sharpened her culinary skills in that establishment. Ethel had an electric, commanding personality. She filled up a room, said one family member; she was admired and loved.

Wali Akbar Muhammad, former photo editor of *Muhammad Speaks* newspaper and editor of *Bilalian News,* was married to the granddaughter of Clara, Ruqaiyah Muhammad. Wali Akbar first met Clara in the 1950s when she visited the residence on Staple Street in Washington, D.C. She was en route to Chicago from her recent trip to Georgia to visit her parents. Wali Akbar, then an assistant minister at Temple #4 Washington, D.C., was assigned to escort Clara wherever she wanted to go around the city. He said of her, as others have; she was regal and gracious. He added, *"She also impressed me as serious and very aware of what was going on…One morning at breakfast, she came down, and naturally I snapped to attention as soon as she came in."* He reported, *"She asked if I had breakfast, and I said, I ate only one meal a day. She looked at me and said, 'Brother, what do you think my husband would say if he knew you were driving me around and you didn't have anything to eat all day.' I was surprised and said, 'I would not want to investigate that kind of situation.' Sister Clara remained silent. I paused and told the sister who was cooking, 'I'll have the scrambled eggs.'"*[116]

When the Staple Street property was sold to a Muslim

member, Wali Akbar Muhammad had another opportunity to witness Clara Muhammad. *"Myself and another brother moved the furniture from the Staple Street property to Chicago at the request of Sister Clara. We delivered the furniture where we were instructed and then went to her residence at 4847 South Woodlawn Avenue. We gave her a fair price for the cost of the truck and the plane ticket back to D.C. She said, 'I know that you probably kept the price down because you were thinking of my husband. I'm going to pay you what you charged us, and then I want you to have this gift.' And she gave an additional $600 to each of us."*[117] Clara exhibited the same generosity when she and Lottie Rayya, the National Captain of the MGT&GCC, visited Boston and encountered the poverty of Minister Louis X (Farrakhan) and his family. Within a short period of time, the Minister received a hand-delivered envelope with $400 inside.

The new home at 4847 South Woodlawn Avenue changed the life of Clara Evans Muhammad for good and ill. At last, she had a dignified home and help to decorate and run it as she chose. The property was an 18-room mansion on the South Side of Chicago. Initially, the neighborhood had been depressed, and properties were traditionally rented as apartments. However, the purchase of the home revitalized that neighborhood of Chicago, and the Muhammad residence became the centerpiece of Muslim progress. The promise of money, good homes, and friendship in all walks of life was reaping tangible results.

With the purchase of the mansion in 1952, Clara's life changed. Her health continued to be a concern, but she was initially able to live a more relaxed life. She did not work outside of the home and received a monthly stipend of an unknown amount from her husband to spend as she pleased. The memory of hunger and the days of starvation greatly influenced how Clara lived when her economic condition improved. She converted the entire basement of the mansion into a warehouse for food which she consistently donated to needy families. *"She canned fruits and vegetables, made jams and jellies, and churned her own butter in her basement,"* reported granddaughter Ruqaiyah, daughter of Clara's eldest son Emmanuel. She lived with her grandmother from the age of four to 18 years of age. *"My grandmother would wake up in the middle of the night and go to her basement to box food for needy families. She would churn her own butter and, when completed, would put designs on top of it and place it in a beautiful crystal butter dish. Sometimes she would wake me up and say, 'Let's make some bread or a cake.' I would join her, and we had the best time."*[118]

As the 1950s progressed, Clara's family rules were consistent from the early days, and her husband agreed with her. Her grandchildren were not to spend the night or eat in anyone's home. Ruqaiyah said, *"My grandparents were serious about our safety but also our behavior. We never went anywhere unescorted; we always had a chaperone."*[119] Many conflated the safety of the Muhammad family with privilege. It was some of both; they were labeled the "Royal Family," and their excesses were a focus. However, when put in context, this is a family who sacrificed and built the Nation of Islam and devoted their lives to its continuance.

New Temples of Islam emerged and expanded in Chicago, Philadelphia, New York, New Jersey, and most cities along the east coast of the United States. The phenomena affected the religious and cultural climate of the Black community and America in general. Preachers and Black middle-class integrationists anxiously watched and consistently rebuked Muslim efforts. They perceived the *Lost Found Nation of Islam* as a direct challenge to Christianity, the philosophy of integration, the Civil Rights Movement, and their relationship with white authority.

Since Elijah's release from prison in 1946, he lived with the scourge of being called a thug and criminal. Such words were famously used in 1959 by Supreme Court Justice Thurgood Marshall in describing him and the Muslim movement. That narrative became a weapon for those who sought to halt the growth of Al-Islam in America, especially Negro leaders ordained by the establishment, who supported integration as a solution to the race problem. In response to Thurgood Marshall, George Schuyler, a Black conservative, wrote in the *Pittsburg Courier*, "*Mr. Muhammad may be a rogue…but when anyone can get tens of thousands of Negroes to practice economic solidarity, respect their women, alter their atrocious diet, give up liquor, stop crime and juvenile delinquency and adultery, he is doing more for Negroes' welfare than any current leader I know.*"[120]

The new language of As-Salaamu-Alaikum became *avant-garde*; although when mangled by those who were not Muslim, it sounded more like salaamsalaykum. It joined the new language of *righteous brother/sister*, *Queen* for the Black woman, *original man*, and *knowledge of self* and *do for self*. Beautiful Black women and fine Black men emerged from the Temples of Islam extending courtesies the poor had seldom experienced. When one entered the Temples or Muslim businesses, the average Black person, who was often disrespected by the higher social classes of their own kind, were endeared by the respect shown by their Muslim Brothers and Sisters. In 1954, Malcolm X became the Minister of Temple #7 in Harlem, New York. Black men began pouring into the Nation of Islam, embracing a newfound identity of manhood. Black women followed them. They married, had babies, and the University of Islam schools and Muslim businesses grew.

In the 1950s and early 1960s, secretarial skills were a premium and one of the most prestigious jobs for women generally. To be an executive secretary in any organization was a sign of success for women. Next to marrying a good Muslim man, one of the greatest aspirations for single women in the *Nation of Islam* was to become a secretary to the Honorable Elijah Muhammad. It was a selective position of high esteem and elevated anyone who could obtain it. It placed one squarely in the inner circle of the messianic leader, and the potential benefits were enormous. Many women sought the position, and some also sought Elijah. The veneration of Clara's husband was witnessed by males and females who openly admitted they would give their life for him.

Clara's decades of struggle and unwavering commitment slowly began to be known, but still only to a few. Emmanuel Muhammad, the eldest child, clarified what his mother did for the *Nation of Islam* in an article in *Muhammad Speaks*. In the following excerpt, he said: *"She held our family together all the while he [Elijah Muhammad] was on the run. And while he was in prison, the remaining officials would seek information from her. She would bring understanding from my father on questions she could not answer – she gathered and sent or brought to my father and me whatever literature the prison permitted. She typed verses from the Holy Qur'an and sent them to us. In general, she held the family together all the while my father was in prison. Even now, she's up late at night to help nurse him in times of illness. She's a living, continual witness to my father as Allah's last and greatest Messenger. When my father and I were in prison, the FBI approached my mother and told her that she would have to return the children to the devil's school. She told them she would rather die first."*[121]

Education and the University of Islam remained Clara's focus. Her children were now grown, and as a grandmother, she could subordinate her strict discipline to her loving heart. Clara had softened, but she still could whip you with her words if she chose. Clarence Walker Muhammad, the son of her sister now named Rose Ameenah, testified. He called Clara "Auntie" and recalled, *"Whatever Auntie said, she put her foot down on it...I took Auntie and a Sister downtown to one of the major department stores. I dropped them off, and she told me what time to come back to pick her up at the corner of Michigan and State Streets. It was cold. I decided I would run an errand but got lost in underground Chicago and kept going around in circles. I was almost an hour late picking her up. She was not a cursing lady and did not curse me. But man, oh man, 'She said, Boy, where have you been? You wait until I get you home. I'm about to freeze, and you're gallivanting around the city'... She stayed at it. What she said to me turned me upside down and inside out. I felt like I had been beat up a thousand times."*[122]

CHAPTER 10: MOTHER TO THINKERS, TEACHERS, AND WARRIORS (JAMES BALDWIN, MALCOLM X, LOUIS X, AND MUHAMMAD ALI)

By the 1960s, the environment in America was rumbling with discontent. Acts of defiance at the establishment were on one extreme and a push for self-determination on the other. The Vietnam War was escalating, and racial oppression towards Black people continued. Yet, a seismic shift was occurring in the identity and behavior of members of the Black community. Muslim women found a new level of respect. Men would move to let them pass on the street, tilt their hats ,and stop unsavory behavior in their presence. Black men were walking with a gait of confidence, their heads erect. The Muslim way of greeting – hugging your brother or sister, hand to hand, cheek to cheek – gained traction and became the way to greet each other. Unity in the Black community increased; Black men were more assertive about marriage and family life as many wanted *one of those good Muslim women who could cook.* Supported by Black Family Day Bazaars and other community activities, the Muslims set a new example for cleanliness, family life, and economic progress.

The purity and virginity of Black women became front and center, exemplified by Muslim women who remained chaste until marriage. Whatever life one previously lived, becoming Muslim brought a new life of purity, and the Nation of Islam stressed, *Where There Are No Decent Women, There Are No Decent Men.* Health, cleanliness, and proper eating became a focus. The act of not eating pork became a badge of intelligence and pride.

Do not eat swine was the colloquial talk in Black neighborhoods. Spurred by the emergence of James Baldwin, Malcolm X, *Muhammad Speaks* newspaper, and Muhammad Ali, the decade of the 1960s catapulted Muslims into college classrooms and living rooms throughout the country. Clara's husband called the Bible the *Poison Book* and cited the Biblical story of Lazarus to describe Black people who loved Caucasians so much that they refused to get up and do something for themselves.

Criticism continued, especially from Christian preachers, but the practical accomplishments of the Muslims could not be denied. Notable thinkers and scholars lauded the University of Islam and the Nation of Islam generally for its ability to provide what no other social institutions in America provided. Writer and social critic James Baldwin made the following statement in 1962: *"Elijah Muhammad has been able to do what generations of welfare workers and committees and resolutions and reports and housing projects and playgrounds have failed to do: to heal and redeem drunkards and junkies, to convert people who have come out of prison and to keep them out, to make men chaste and women virtuous and to invest both the male and the female with pride and a serenity that hang about them like an unfailing light. He has done all these things, which our Christian church has spectacularly failed to do. How has Elijah managed it?"*[123]

Baldwin did not come into the Nation of Islam but noted in his book, *The Fire Next Time*, how much he was impressed with not only his conversation with Elijah Muhammad but the ambiance of his home. There was a peace and tranquility he felt in the environment, the quiet presence and dignity of the women, and the delicious food. Each of those elements spoke to Clara Muhammad. Although unknown to Baldwin and the general public, the majority of the membership of the Nation of Islam were not social deviants. They were former church people dissatisfied with a Christian theology that deemed them less than human beings and a better life only after death.

The new home at 4847 S. Woodlawn Avenue was filled with family. Elijah's sister, Annie, lived in the mansion as did other family and grandchildren periodically. Clara's children were now adults, all married, some more than once, providing numerous opportunities for her to offer mother guidance. She was not an interfering mother-in-law, reported several of her children and Harriet Muhammad-Abu Bakr, who was once married to Akbar. If she observed something blatant, she would respond. Otherwise, she waited to be invited into the marital matters of her children.

The purchase of the 18-room mansion by Elijah established new traditions. A large picture of W. D. Fard Muhammad greeted all visitors upon entering the home. Dinner was served at exactly 4:00 p.m. daily in the dining room. The Minister of Temple #2 and head Laborers reported to dinner every Sunday to deliver reports. Serious table talk and meetings with significant people around dinner were the new norms. Clara's husband sat at the head of the table, and she always sat at his right side. It was a formal environment with white linen table cloths and napkins, the best china, and gold-plated cutlery. A smaller table was also in the main dining room where the secretaries ate. A table in the breakfast nook off the kitchen was for younger children, if necessary. Clara was the Mother of the Nation and had a keen perch to observe those who came to the mansion – as it was called – to meet with her husband, the Honorable Elijah Muhammad.

Clara was inspired by Elijah's plan to build a 20-million-dollar education, hospital, and business complex in Chicago, one of the biggest and most aggressive projects of her husband. The proposal was reported in *Muhammad Speaks* and all of the local Chicago newspapers. Its goal was to transform the Southside of Chicago and elevate the status of Muslims and the larger Black community. Clara relished an expanded program for the University of Islam that would educate more children with state-of-the-art facilities. However, Negro preachers, integrationists, and powerful forces in and out of Chicago organized and undermined the project. The land designated was cleared but was eventually turned into a playground with no hospital, businesses, or educational facilities for the failed Black population on the South Side of Chicago. Although unsuccessful in that venture, the Muslims' ambitions and their growing impact on the cultural and religious climate in America made J. Edgar Hoover's FBI surveillance, which began in 1931, unrelenting.

Clara continued to organize her household and made several trips to Cordele, Georgia, in the early 1960s to address the failing health of her mother and father. The growth of the Nation of Islam and the organization and administration of its affairs became more complex. The mansion became the official workplace of her husband, and several secretaries were hired. Initially, Clara played a central role in organizing the staff.

She also organized and supervised her household staff. She and her staff managed members of the MGT&GCC, including her granddaughters, who were taught to serve the numerous guests who came to the mansion. Unless Elijah requested something specific, she planned all the meals for the household and guests. She organized food purchases delivered to her from the farm via the Muslim grocery store. Elijah himself was an excellent cook, say the children and grandchildren, but Clara was a superior cook. Her husband preferred her cooking and frequently requested it. She was particular about her kitchen, and one had to be invited in. If one were so fortunate, she would often share some recipes and her special touch to the Muslim bean soup.

Fern Tauheedah Mahmoud and Shakeelah Hassan were some of the few who were privileged to be in Clara's presence in the kitchen. Fern Tauheedah Mahmoud reported, *"Sister Clara never used tomato paste in her bean soup; she used fresh tomatoes."*[124] Her granddaughters Halimah Muhammad-Ali and Ruqaiyah Muhammad-Farrar reported that Clara cooked everything fresh, no canned foods. She would cook in bulk and either can her items or freeze them. She mastered the basic traditional Muslim recipes of bean soup, whole wheat bread, bean pie, carrot cake, carrot pie, squash pies, etc. She learned to make baklava, stuffed eggplant, and various delicious dishes that the family often requested. Clara also made special health drinks for herself and her husband, consisting of carrots and apples and a green drink of spinach, celery, green peppers, and other items.

Minister Louis Farrakhan recalled the Honorable Elijah Muhammad and Sister Clara visiting Boston for a program he arranged in 1958. He said, *"I got out of my bed and Mother Clara and the Honorable Elijah Muhammad stayed in that bed and security was around them. The next day, my wife was in the kitchen cooking with other MGT; they thought the honor would be theirs to cook for the Honorable Elijah Muhammad and his wife. Mother Clara Muhammad said 'No! Sister Betsy you cook for your husband but I'm cooking for mine.' She had brought food up to the apartment and was teaching my wife what kind of pots she should have. Not aluminum pots, but stainless steel. So, Sister Clara cooked for her husband."*[125]

The household staff of Clara were loyal Muslims from the early days who loved her and her husband and also understood her health challenges. As a result of Clara's surgery, she could only eat small soft food meals and had to consume crème to coat her stomach before eating. Few knew of her health issues, and she would not eat those small meals in public so as not to contradict the policy of one meal-a-day espoused by the Nation of Islam. Her two main cooks, Sisters Earlene and Francis, knew her condition. Later, Lana Shabazz, who cooked for Muhammad Ali, would cook for her and become a confidant. Clara would often visit Lana in Florida, where her brothers Carlton and Willie also lived. Sister Francis and her husband, Brother Albert, the grounds caretaker, looked after Clara very well.

In the early 1960s, Clara's Sister Rosalie accepted Islam, changed her name to Rose Ameenah Muhammad, and moved into the mansion. Eventually, the son of Rose Ameenah, Clarence, and his wife, Geneva, lived on the grounds from 1961 to 1971 and became a part of the household staff. Geneva helped in the house and cooked; Clarence drove the *Muhammad*

Speaks newspaper tractor-trailer, delivering papers nationwide and items from the Michigan farm to the Muslim supermarket. He recalled, *"If my Auntie ran out of items, I would take her to the Farmers Market on the Dan Ryan [Expressway] in Chicago. The people there knew her and would say, 'Mrs. Muhammad, what can we get for you today?'"*[126]

Away from the limelight, Clara remained a mother to the Nation. She nurtured the children of the first Muslim pioneers, including Gloria, the daughter of her friend and confidant Viola Karriem. Gloria worked in Clara's home and helped in numerous ways. Darnell Kariem, the son of another pioneer who served in prison with her husband, wanted to marry Gloria. He grew up with Clara's children and was always at the house. He reported, *"I delivered pastries from the Muslim Grocery and Bakery but found it difficult to save my money. I wanted to marry Gloria but knew I had to have my money in place. I talked to Sister Clara about it, and she assisted me taking a portion of my weekly earnings and saving it for me."*[127] Darnell and Gloria eventually married, and Clara had a cache of money to give them when she attended their wedding, along with her gift of a vacuum cleaner. Clara also financially supported struggling families and made scholarships available to students at the University of Islam. Her keen observation was to see where help was needed and to provide it.

When Clara met Malcolm X, she liked him immediately. She agreed to have Lottie Rayya travel with Malcolm X. As he set up Temples in the eastern United States, she set up MGT&GCC for Muslim women. The more Clara saw and observed Malcolm, her affection for him grew. It is reported that she said that Malcolm X was good and sincere and dedicated to helping her husband. She called him a son. *"Malcolm made my grandmother laugh; he was a jokester. He was always happy and pleasant, and he loved her cooking,"* reported granddaughter Ruqaiyah Muhammad-Farrar. Halimah Muhammad-Ali, another granddaughter, said, *"When Malcolm came to the mansion, grandmother would personally prepare his plate and would pile it to the rim because she knew he only ate one meal a day. When he finished that first plate of food, she would have another ready for him. Grandmother really loved him and was deeply hurt when he was killed. She never believed Grandfather had anything to do with it. They both became gravely ill after Malcolm was assassinated to the point that doctors had to be called. They were deeply hurt."*[128]

As Mother of the Nation, Clara exercised her role with considerable personal liberty. Her inherent skill was to weave numerous concerns into a single effort so that peace and progress prevailed. In the face of many challenges, Clara was silent but not absent. The weight of her persona was light but powerful. She could zero in on a problem with surgical precision, analyze the issue, apply correction and healing and withdraw, leaving the patient often speechless but grateful. She was a powerful woman. Yet, those who knew her were convinced that her power came from a source beyond herself. Clara was perceived as a vessel being used to do divine work. She was a woman of faith and gave considerable time to contemplation and prayer.

In an interview, Minister Louis Farrakhan recalled Clara Muhammad's *Mother Leadership* in the late 1950s. He said, *"My first encounter with Mother, I call her Mother because she is and was the Mother of the Nation of Islam even though we didn't always use that language. But looking back at her, she was the Mother of our Nation and the MGT...When I first met her, I was the Honorable Elijah Muhammad's Captain in Boston, Massachusetts, and I was blessed to speak as a Captain. I became a Minister in May 1957. By Saviour's Day 1958, I was, of course, in Chicago, and I and my wife, Khadijah, she was Betsy X at that time, were invited to the home of the Honorable Elijah Muhammad. And when Mother Clara Muhammad saw my wife's shoes – run down and run over – she called me to the side and in a motherly way chastised me. She said: Look how nice you look and look at your wife's shoes. She said it would be better if you came in coveralls and your wife and your children were dressed up. That would show you as a good, hard-working father and a good husband. But to come looking as you look and your wife has run-over shoes, that doesn't look well for you,*

Brother Minister. So she went in her purse and gave my wife some money to go out and buy some new shoes."[129]

Clara liked Muhammad Ali and his affable boyish charm. He often came to the mansion with his soon-to-be wife, Belinda Ali (Khalilah Camacho Ali). Khalilah said, *"Muhammad came from a good home with loving parents, but it was Sister Clara Muhammad who helped refine his manners. She was the one who showed him that bread and butter should be on a plate, not on the table."*[130] Her granddaughter Halimah Muhammad-Ali also added, *"Grandmother was the one who helped Ali understand the proper use of the different cutlery at the table setting."*

As the now commonly called Nation of Islam grew in respect, people of all sorts wanted to know more about it, especially traditional Muslims who believed it was their responsibility to correct the *aberrant* Nation. Shakeelah and Zia Hassan, a married couple at the University of Chicago Medical School, were one such couple. Born in India and raised in Pakistan, they raised theological issues with the Muhammads and had impassioned discussions that proved instructive for all. Shakeelah came to respect the intelligence of Clara Muhammad and her husband and their unique path to Al-Islam. As understandings grew, they regarded Clara and her husband as surrogate parents and began numerous cultural exchanges as compassionate human beings.

Shakeelah Hassan said when interviewed, *"Sister Clara was nothing short of a mother to me. Whatever she did, she always understood herself to be setting an example for others—from the way she meticulously arranged the contents of her purse and attended to the minutest details of keeping a clean home – 'where the angels would feel welcome' – to the loving way in which she prepared meals for her family and guests. As dignified a woman as she was, however, she was never stiff or aloof. My fondest memories are her teaching me how to make her famous navy bean soup—something I make to this day for her grandchildren who are like children to me."*[131]

Shakeelah Hassan also takes responsibility for making

the famous fez that graced the head of Clara's husband, Elijah. She says, *"It was a labor of love and an expression of appreciation for the work of two dearly beloved people."*[132] (The grandson of Clara, Hasan Sharif, says, *"My mother, Ethel, was the first to make a fez for my Grampa. I remember her staying up nights sewing those stones and ornaments on his fez."*[133])

Shakeelah Hassan continues, *"Sometime in the late 1950s, he [Elijah Muhammad] said that he wanted a special hat for a special occasion – a fez. As we talked, I drew a hat on a piece of paper, combining an Indian/ Pakistani style with symbols of the Nation of Islam, a star, and crescent with other stars throughout the design. I bought beautiful velvet fabric from Marshall Field department store and sent it to friends in Lahore [Pakistan] who embroidered it to my specification. It was the first of many we had made in a variety of colors."*[134]

The Hassan's relationship was proof of what Clara and her husband Elijah were saying to the world. They were living the promise made by W. D. Fard Muhammad: *Money, good homes, and friendship in all walks of life.*

PART 5: A BREACH IN THE NATION OF ISLAM

CHAPTER 11: MARITAL RIGHT OR MARITAL RISK

As the decade advanced, Clara's life became a paradox: joyful at the success of the Honorable Elijah Muhammad and devastated at her relationship with her husband. *"That is how she often spoke,"* said her first grandchild, Hasan Sharif. *"My grandmother referred to my grandfather as my husband."*[135] But Clara looked at her husband's work through the title he gave himself, Messenger of Allah. She could separate his unprecedented accomplishments on behalf of the Black man and woman in America from his personal behavior, and still support the program of the Honorable Elijah Muhammad. But by 1963, the fifty-four-year union of head and heart was strained. Clara and her husband had weathered some of the most turbulent experiences, but always together. The new challenges, however, were splitting them apart.

It was a unique marriage with heretofore unbreakable bonds. Clara loved Elijah, and Elijah loved Clara. She stood him up when he needed support, was compassionate when he doubted himself, took him to meet W. D. Fard Muhammad, protected his back when trouble came, stood beside him during rough times, and stood on his behalf as he fled adversaries and was imprisoned. She nursed his illnesses, birthed and raised eight children almost single-handed, taught them to love and respect him even in his absence. She raised money to bail him out of jail and protected his dignity in the eyes of his family and the Nation of Islam. He was the only man in her life from the age of seventeen. Clara Muhammad believed in him and his mission and was unquestionably his best follower and supporter. Even with the stressors in the marriage, there was a cordial acknowledgment of respect and appreciation.

Granddaughters Halimah Muhammad-Ali and Amirah Muhammad both said, *"Grandmother also called him 'EM', and he called her 'girl'."* One of the early followers, Hafeesah Al Uqdah, who moved to Los Angeles, recalled, "I think they were really, cute. He would do what he wanted to do, and she would do what she wanted to do. And if it looked like he got out of control, she would pull him right back in." However, Clara's pull became less effective as Elijah was changing.

Clara's husband became distant, argumentative, and insensitive, and gave his wife practically no time or attention. Called by his devoted followers "the Honorable Elijah Muhammad", he was solidly established, admired, loved, and influential. The passing of his mother, Marie, in August 1957 represented the removal of the last parental figure in his life. Marie would tell stories of his childhood, citing how they called him "Prophet". And although he was small in frame, she believed he had a great destiny, as he was spiritually sensitive, always his own authority, and answerable to no one but himself. In 1959, he traveled to parts of the historically Muslim world and performed *Umrah,* which is completing the rites of the Muslim pilgrimage of Hajj, but outside of the designated season. It is believed that this trip and the passing of his mother had a significant influence on his decisions going forward.

Clara's husband witnessed the reality of the Muslim world after its colonial onslaught, seeing it as disappointing and disillusioning with poverty, smoking, drinking, corruption, dictators, and racism rampant. Her husband believed G-D empowered him to bring in a new Islam, led by the former enslaved. His actions indicated that he intended to multiply his seed in that new order. Other family members said, *"He was a man, not divine, but a man with weaknesses that spilled over into relationships with younger women. He was still young, handsome, and powerful, and could do what he wanted."* How Elijah addressed his wants and weakness shattered Clara and left a trail of devastation that compromised his honor and breached the Nation of Islam.

The physical health of Clara was challenged, but more so was her emotional health. She was now 58 years old, past childbearing years, with a severe stomach condition that was painful and potentially debilitating. The depth of her role as Mother of the Nation and her endless sacrifices and support of the Honorable Elijah Muhammad remained unappreciated by most outsiders and newer members. But irrespective of the emotional distance between her husband and herself, Clara remained his most ardent supporter. Wherever Clara went, she promoted the Honorable Elijah Muhammad and his program, not herself. Yet, her level of support, often overlooked or taken for granted, was so essential that one could make the argument that there would not be an Honorable Elijah Muhammad without Clara. She supported, protected, and stabilized him; she raised his children, who provided leadership to the Nation of Islam. She was the heart of the Muhammad family, and if she was unhappy, it was felt by all family members.

Clara's mother, Mary Lou Thomas Evans, passed in 1959, and Clara went to Cordele, Georgia to be with her family for the funeral. Within a year, Mamie, Clara's oldest sister, also died. She again traveled to attend the funeral along with Lottie Rayya and her son and Ethel and her daughter. Her father's health became a concern, and she did not want to leave Quartus alone in Cordele.

A popular Minister of Clara's husband was Jeremiah Shabazz. He had been designated the first Captain of the FOI in Philadelphia by Malcolm X when Malcolm supervised the Philadelphia Temple of Islam at 1619 Bailey Street. Clara's husband sent Jeremiah Shabazz to Atlanta in 1959 as Minister of the southern region. He and his wife, Elizabeth, the first Sister Captain in Philadelphia, stayed in Atlanta for eight years through the Civil Rights Movement. Their proximity to Clara and Elijah's hometown became significant. When Clara visited her family, she would first go to Atlanta, and Jeremiah Shabazz would personally escort her to Cordele. Clara and Elizabeth developed a mother-daughter relationship. Elizabeth Shabazz said, *"Clara's mother and sister died while we were in Atlanta, and she did not want to leave her father alone. Jeremiah brought Quartus back to Atlanta, and he lived with us for approximately two years. Jeremiah really had a way with older people and young people; it was the ones in between that he didn't care much for."*[136] Why Clara did not immediately move her father to her home in Chicago can only be speculated.

A confluence of events in 1962 brought a nagging disturbance Clara experienced for years confronting her face-to-face with a reality so devastating she thought she would die. The infiltration of the FBI into the Nation of Islam remains culpable in delivering distress to the well-being of Clara Muhammad. Since 1930, to destroy *the Lost Found Nation of Islam* and reveal its weaknesses, J. Edgar Hoover had hounded the Nation of Islam. Now, under the COINTEL Program, he installed agents posing as Muslims and tapped the telephones of Clara, Elijah, and Nation of Islam leaders. Agents also compiled and sent graphic letters to Clara outlining her husband's indiscretions beginning in 1962. Subsequent letters were sent to Clara's daughters, Ethel and Lottie Rayya, and other Nation officials. The indiscretions were described as adulterous affairs with several of his secretaries and the fathering of children with them. The letter writing was so egregious that even today some remain redacted in FBI files. FBI documents also disclosed that for years Clara suspected her husband of infidelity. As early as 1955-56, there were whispers within the family of her husband's indiscretions with a female relative and possibly another child. Inside the residence at 4847 S. Woodlawn Avenue, Clara observed behavior that raised her suspicions. Outside the home, there was evidence.

On July 3, 1962, United Press International sent a wire to radio and television stations across the United States that read: *"Elijah Muhammad, a 67 year old leader of the Black Muslim movement, today faced paternity suits from two former secretaries who charged he fathered their four children... Both women are in their twenties.... Miss [Evelyn] Williams and Miss [Lucille] Rosary charged they had intimacies with Elijah Muhammad from 1957 until this year [1962]. Miss [Lucille] Rosary alleged he fathered her two children and said she was expecting a third child by him....the other plaintiff said he was the father of her daughter....."*

Malcolm X heard the announcement, but the women in question had been put out of the Nation, and anyone in the Nation was prohibited from speaking with them. Malcolm is reported to have said that he encountered a young woman who said she had a child by the Honorable Elijah Muhammad and had been put out of the Nation of Islam. Conducting his own investigation, he spoke to several women who presented similar circumstances. He then wrote in his autobiography, *"...I broke the rule that no Muslim is supposed to have any contact with another Muslim in the 'isolated' state. I looked up, and I talked with three of the former secretaries to Mr. Muhammad. From their own mouths, I heard their stories of who had fathered their children."*[137] An official paternity suit was filed, July 2, 1964.

After his mother Marie's passing, by the early 1960s Elijah had established another office in a newly acquired apartment complex at 8205 S. Vernon Avenue, Chicago. Several of his secretaries were given apartments in the residence, and Elijah frequently spent long hours there described as work. FBI documents reported he spent many nights there, although some male family members continue to dispute that. FBI records also reported that at their Phoenix, Arizona, residence at 2118 E. Violet Drive, Clara overheard her husband in a romantic telephone conversation with one of his secretaries while another attended him at the residence under circumstances she believed breached her marriage. Elijah promised to buy the woman on the telephone a diamond ring. Clara was incensed. The wiretapping revealed what she essentially said to him and later confessed to her daughters, Ethel and Lottie Rayya. She was fed up with his behavior and sweet talk to other women while treating her like a dog. Male family members again disagreed, stating he would not dare have such a conversation with another woman with Clara in close proximity.

Yet, in what appeared to be a direct response to Clara's protestations, Elijah Muhammad, Jr. said, *"In the early 1960s, I took my mother to get a wedding ring. Yes, I took her because my father never gave her one because they could not afford it until later years. About ten years before she passed, in 1962, he told me to take her downtown and buy her a ring. I took her to Marshall Field. She did not spend the money he gave her to get it with; she bought something simple, she did not buy anything expensive. Both of them were like that. My father would get clothes, spend $39 for a suit or something. He would not buy a suit for $85 - $100. He did not do that. She picked out a little gold band, white gold with a little maybe ¼ of a carat diamond. It was just simple. She did not want anything. And she had the money. She was not concerned with flashy clothes and jewelry. That was not her, and that was not him."*[138]

What appeared to be rapprochement did not last. Elijah's behavior continued, and Clara's sadness increased. Clara's grandson Hasan Sharif said, *"He should have taken her [to get her first wedding ring] or better, my uncle could have taken both of them."* Hasan Sharif believed the insensitivity of his grandfather contributed to the overwhelming sadness Clara was already experiencing. What could have been a healing moment produced more distance and insensitivity.

In 1963, it was reported that Elijah Muhammad had fathered thirteen children with seven women. The FBI documents disclosed that the mothers of the children had requested additional money, but Elijah refused. Some threatened to go public, Elijah dared them and discredited them, resulting in several women being put out of the Nation of Islam. Then came the event that brought Clara indescribable pain.

Before Saviour's Day 1963, some of the women Clara perceived as mistresses came to the house at 4847 S. Woodlawn Avenue, Chicago. Family members say the doorbell rang. Hasan Sharif, the first grandchild who lived in the mansion with his wife, Nniyyah, opened the door. *"I remember Ola, Lucille, and Evelyn, three women were on the porch with at least three or four children. They were toddlers. The women turned around and left the children at the door. They said nothing. The babies were crying. I called my mother, Ethel Muhammad Sharrieff; she brought the children into the house. This is when I found out Grandfather had fathered children with these women. At least two other women were standing beside a car parked in front of the house.*[139]

"*Within fifteen minutes after the children were in the house, the doorbell rang again. When I opened the door, Minister Malcolm was standing there. He said to me, 'Salaamayakum, Hasan, is everything alright?' After a pause, I said yes. He said, 'Are you sure Hasan? If everything is not alright, I will feel bad if I cannot help.' I told him everything was alright. He then said, 'Hasan, you are like Peter at the gate.' My grandfather was up in his room, and I believe saw all that happened out of his window.*"[140]

"*My mother took charge of the children and tried to keep them from Grandmother. In an effort to shield my grandfather, my father, Supreme Captain Raymond Sharrieff, took the children and, when later questioned by the press, said they were his. When my mother Ethel heard that, she exploded. She got so mad with my father she literally jumped all over him.*"[141]

As expected, Clara learned of the incident. It was reported that when she saw the children, she was horrified. Citing letters sent by the FBI, subtle disrespect from secretaries in her home, and crying children at her door, Clara confronted Elijah. He admitted to his involvement with other women and children outside of the marriage. Clara left the bedroom she shared with her husband and moved into the bedroom that Mother Marie previously occupied. The day the children were deposited at her home, Clara stayed in that room weeping. She spoke with her children Ethel, Lottie Rayya, Wallace, and Emmanuel about the incidents. With the conduct of her husband and the secretaries around her, she felt violated in her own home. Each child interviewed expressed hurt observing their mother's pain and came to her defense. They did not confront their father, the Honorable Elijah Muhammad however.

Grandson Hasan Sharif explains, "*No one confronted him*

about his behavior. It just was. When he wanted to, he would speak to his sons individually about it. We were hurt because it was our grandmother, and to tell you the truth, we had some resentment, but he was the Honorable Elijah Muhammad, and in our mind and his, he was responsible to no one but himself, although he would say Allah. It was a situation we knew existed, and it just was. The women in the family felt more depth of hurt than the men, but no one got in his face and said this is wrong. So here is the paradox, the pretzel logic: He was weak, had these relationships; tried to hide them, then tried to justify them with his prophetic role, yet he loved grandmother."[142]

Clara stayed in her room. She sat in the rocking chair of Mother Marie, looking out of the window of the mansion that she once was so pleased to move into. The happiness and pleasure were gone, and all she could do was contemplate her life. *"I loved my grandmother,"* said Hasan Sharif. *"I used to visit her. If she was not taking a nap, she would take a walk or be reading a book. She tried to keep herself busy. Otherwise, she would be in her room in her chair. We would talk. She had a quiet dignity about herself, but after the revelations of the women, I noticed something missing in her eyes. She was bearing all of this stuff about the secretaries and still supporting Grandfather's leadership. She was still cordial to him. They exchanged nice words. '...How are you today?' 'Fine.' 'How are you doing today?' Sometimes he would kiss her on the cheek, you know. So with all of that, and you see he has babies by this one and that one, as a youngster you just kind of...I was in my early 20's."*

Nathaniel Muhammad, the second eldest son, said, *"My mother was the best that my Daddy had. She let Daddy do anything he wanted to do. She would never let you talk about him or it [his indiscretions], question him, or say anything negative about him. Because I didn't like it when he got all those women. I'll tell you the truth; I didn't like it. And I let my mother know it. But you know what she told me? She said, 'Son, shut up. Allah will punish you if you talk about your father.' And I shut up just like she said. But I was hurt. But she would never let me say anything negative about him."*[143]

Two women (Evelyn Williams and Lucile Rosary) filed a paternity suit against Elijah Muhammad in 1964.[144] Years later, in 1975, a lawsuit was filed against the estate of Elijah Muhammad by three of his children.[145] Emmanuel Muhammad, the eldest son, was called to testify in court in 1978. He was asked:

Question: Did you have a conversation with your father concerning whether he was the father of those [thirteen] children?
Emmanuel: Later, I came into the knowledge of that. Later on, not right away, that they were his children and also my brothers and sisters.
Question: When you say later, what do you mean, sir, in point of time?
Emmanuel: He tried to keep it a secret from the family.[146]

But even as far back as 1962, emotional distance grew, and spats between Clara and Elijah escalated. During one uncomfortable exchange, he essentially told Clara to get out. She would take brief trips to Florida to visit her brother Carlton who lived with her in Chicago during 1967-68. However, she decided she needed more distance. Clara decided to travel to Egypt to visit her son Akbar. Accompanied by her son Herbert, it was her first travel out of the country. She welcomed the new environment away from the stressors of Elijah, the painful letters from the FBI, and the secretaries. Akbar and his new wife, Harriet, welcomed her.

Harriet recalled, *"I believe Clara's first trip to Egypt was something she wanted to do for herself. She had always carried the load of the Nation. She didn't venture too far from home, not on her own or for her pleasure. As she started to get older, and with the challenges she was faced with, she just wanted to take a break and get some time for herself. So she did that with us in Cairo.*

Herbert stayed about three days, and Clara stayed approximately one month. We toured the city, visited historic sites, cooked and ate great food, and when she returned to Chicago, she was in a better frame of mind."[147]

As the Nation of Islam population increased, so did the operations at home. Clara was no longer responsible for the tasks she had managed when her husband was fleeing and imprisoned. Her previous responsibilities were given to others, and a new chain of command was established that reported directly to her husband or someone designated by him. Clara did retain some responsibility for the collection of monies for bank deposits. Delores Daimah Jordan was the daughter of Calvin Jordan, the first manager of the farmland in Michigan. She served as a secretary to Clara's husband and worked with Clara. She said, *"Sister Clara complimented me often and said, I like it when you count the money because you always get it right."*[148] Clara also collected monies from Silas Muhammad, the supervisor for *Muhammad Speaks* newspaper. She showed her support for Silas by baking him a special pie when he was falsely accused of misappropriating 50 dollars from *Muhammad Speaks* monies.

Specific departments were dispersed between eight secretaries who shared a huge office on the 3rd floor of the mansion. Two other secretaries had smaller offices. In some instances, women were in top positions and delivered instructions directly to male leaders from the Honorable Elijah Muhammad. The secretaries' presence, which was initially respectful, became torturous for Clara. Some of Elijah's new children were permitted in the home, and their mothers charged Sister Francis, the cook, with putting harmful ingredients in their food. Sister Francis denied it, but Elijah fired her and told her husband to divorce her. She and Brother Albert had been loyal workers for decades.

"It was hard on her," said her grandson Hasan Sharif. *"You have these women in your house. Some of them look at you like they don't like you. Some look at you like they are ashamed of what they're doing. Some of them are trying to make*

trouble and trying to make you jealous."[149] The invisibility of the Mother of the Nation grew. Her perceived invisibility was confirmed by her at numerous dinner meetings regardless of who was in attendance. It was reported by her granddaughter Ruqaiyyah Muhammad-Farrar that Clara often said, *"I get no respect. If it had not been for me, things would not be the way they are now."*[150] Ruqaiyyah Muhammad-Farrar continued, *"My grandmother knew in her heart and mind that she was responsible for us being Muslims."*[151]

Regardless of what she was experiencing, Clara kept her eye on Wallace. He was teaching from The Qur'an in Philadelphia and had a significant but quiet following. His development appeared to be on track as he stressed spiritual wisdom and human development from The Qur'an. He wrote an article in the September 1960 edition of *Muhammad Speaks* newspaper titled, *"Impact of Islam on Muslim Women"* and said, *"Among the Muslims, the training of men and women is given equal attention because The Qur'an makes women the equal of men...They excel each other in some respects, yet they are equal in the sight of G-D."*[152] Few could take issue with his Qur'anic knowledge, yet several ministers of the Nation of Islam resented his emphasis on The Qur'an rather than Lesson #1 or Lesson #2 for the Supreme Wisdom from W. D. Fard Muhammad. Nevertheless, Wallace persevered.

Forces in the culture, particularly the media, continued to pigeonhole Clara's husband as a hater of Caucasians, even though he had many business dealings with Caucasians and Christians and bought property from Jews. Her husband had already set the stage for cooperation with Caucasians and others, although they were not permitted in the Temple for reasons previously mentioned. Nevertheless, followers were told to respect all people, not even carry a penknife, and only fight with those who fight with you.

The integrationists, led by Black preachers, the Negro Bourgeoisie, and heads of national organizations, i.e., the NAACP, National Urban League, etc., were appealing to white

America for compassion while Clara's husband was appealing to Black America for courage – to stand and build institutions for themselves. As the Civil Rights Movement progressed, the contrasts were stark. Dogs attacked elderly women and children, Black men were battered with billy clubs, and water cannons assaulted young and old, male and female in the name of civil rights – integration: *Let me be a part of your world; sit next to you and attend your schools.* The indignities were emotionally challenging to manage as they were broadcast on television. The voice of Malcolm X consistently narrated events stating that Muslims would not permit their mothers, wives, and children to be attacked in such a manner. He echoed Clara's husband: Black people needed to pool their resources and build their own schools, businesses, and nation.

There was no public discussion of what the integrationists were really thinking behind the scenes. Still, decades later, memorialized in the landmark Public Broadcasting Service (PBS) documentary, *"This Far By Faith,"* Reverend James H. Cone, creator of Black Liberation Theology, said out loud what most Christian preachers, integrationists, and national leaders were silently thinking in the 1960s: *"See, it's important for us to understand that the Nation of Islam was the only religious community of Black people who were unashamed of being Black. Now with that proclamation being so strong and with separatism as a dimension of that proclamation where Black people don't have to be with white people in order to be full human beings, that hit the Civil Rights Movement and the mainstream Black church movement really hard and it shocked us. Because the dominant ethos in the 50s and the early 60s, the first half of it anyway, the dominant ethos was integration. Which means assimilating and going into white institutions, even white churches, etc., white schools, white everything. Now, here was Malcolm and the Nation of Islam saying NO to that. Well, that was frightening to us because deep down, we knew they were telling the truth, but we did not want to hear that truth."*[153]

Reflecting on better times, Elizabeth Shabazz, widow of

Jeremiah Shabazz, who cared for Clara's father in their home, recalled, *"Clara loved Saviour's Day. I would visit Mother Clara at her home in Chicago and remember Saviour's Day was special for her. Jeremiah was a Captain before he was a minister and used to drill the brothers. She loved to see the competitions between the FOI drill teams. That brought a big smile to her face. I remember her being the cleanest, most organized person I ever met. She ironed everything she washed, including dish towels. She was totally devoted to her husband and children."*[154]

Elizabeth Shabazz recalled, *"In 1963, I had a conversation with Mother Clara. I was saying how wonderful things were in Atlanta, and somehow death came up, and I said something to the effect that nothing was worse than death."* Clara is reported to have said, *"Girl, she used to call me girl, some things can happen to you in life that are more painful than death."*[155] Elizabeth said Clara did not elaborate, and she did not follow up on her statement, but the weight of her statement left a heavy feeling in the room. *"Later, when I learned what was going on with the secretaries, and believe me, I was shocked because I thought I knew what was going on in the Nation. When I next saw her, I could see the stress on her face. When Mother Clara stayed over with us, she would get up and make that 5 a.m. prayer. Unfortunately, I did not always do that. On one occasion, I overheard her. Just listening to her pray was overwhelming. I don't want to share what she was saying; it is too private, but it was heart-wrenching."*[156]

Clara was faced with whether her husband's behavior was a marital right or a marital risk. Although the Nation of Islam was in the early stages of Islamic development, high moral behavior was stressed, and The Qur'an was read by her, her husband, and many others. Marriage, secular and religious, requires at least two witnesses and a public announcement. The requirements provide protection and dignity for women, children, and society. Building healthy families was a primary focus of the Nation of Islam, and polygyny, the practice of a man having more than one wife, was unheard of among the majority membership and discouraged by those who understood it.

Nevertheless, it was practiced by a handful of men, though rarely appropriately.

After the domestic issues of Clara's husband became public, the incidences of polygyny increased with disastrous consequences for women, children, and the reputation of the Nation of Islam. Paradoxically, in the larger Black community, the two major obstacles between Black women and the Nation of Islam were covering their bodies and polygyny. Many women feared it and believed a man having an affair was easier to accept than having more than one wife. What was misunderstood is that when properly executed, polygyny protects women and children and makes men responsible for their actions. It is not a license for lustful and immoral behavior, which adultery is. It is also not a license to publicly humiliate the wife if she disagrees with her husband's having more than one wife.

In Al-Islam, polygyny is permitted under certain circumstances, although it remains misunderstood and misused by men and women. The Qur'an, Chapter 4:3, Al Nissa (The Women), says: *"If you fear that you shall not be able to deal justly with the orphans, marry women of your choice, two or three or four: But if you fear that you shall not be able to deal justly with them, then only one, or a captive that your right hand possesses. That will be more suitable to prevent you from doing injustice."*[157] An additional consideration is in Chapter 2:228, Al Baqarah (The Cow or Heifer). It says, *"And women have rights similar to the rights against them according to what is equitable."* [158]

Therefore, if divorce is considered (because a husband wants to practice polygyny), a wife has the right to know before *Talaq* (declaration of divorce) is pronounced and *Iddah* (period of waiting to determine pregnancy) is declared. Polygyny is not a right of the man to be forced upon the woman. She should be made aware of the man's intention to engage in the practice and should be informed of such by him because the practice also affects her. Having such consultation with the wife is equitable behavior. The man is not to ask her permission. The Creator has permitted for men. However, he is required to state his intention so the wife can determine if that is a life she chooses to live.

Clara did not have such a conversation with her husband in advance of his actions. She was not notified of his intention to take additional wives and did not receive an announcement of a marriage or witness any marriage ceremony. She was unaware that he saw other women or that children had been conceived with other women. Therefore, Clara Muhammad did not accept the women as wives but as mistresses. It was this lack of her acceptance of them as wives that resulted in what those close to Clara described as harassment or pestering from them. It also resulted in Elijah's anger at her.

Even though the women had a relationship and children with her husband, the circumstances under which the relationships occurred diminished their status and his in the Nation of Islam and the general public. Validation by Clara would have mitigated that disfavor for some, at least among the Muslims. Thus, the women made numerous efforts to get in her face, trying to force her to acknowledge them as wives of her husband. The positioning ranged from wanting to sit next to her during Saviour's Day and other public ceremonies to requests to visit her at the mansion (4847 S. Woodlawn) outside of regular work hours and for her to see their children. This ultimately led to verbal confrontations in the presence of others where they would seek to define their status as equal to hers. This finagling proved difficult, adding to her emotional challenges of sickness and aging.

Whatever mental and emotional state Clara's husband was experiencing vis-à-vis his messianic position, it is believed he looked at the life of all of the Prophets and felt entitled to certain prerogatives, similar to his prerogative to deify W. D. Fard Muhammad. However, the concern of many was that his rationale came after his actions. The Honorable Elijah Muhammad made no public announcement of marriage to any of the other women. If so, such action would have provided a dignified cover of Islamic marital rights. He also did not marry according to the laws of the State of Illinois. Doing so would have made him vulnerable to the charge of bigamy and the risk of being jailed, something J. Edgar Hoover and the FBI would have appreciated. Elijah Muhammad had no intention of returning to jail.

Therefore, the covert behavior, denial of responsibility in some instances, and the denigration of some of the women diminished the dignity polygyny provides. The narratives of divine seed, prophetic privileges, virgin women, and special children who could see the future in water were floated by ministers of the Nation of Islam and some of the women themselves to mitigate the damage. A few in the public accepted the narratives; most did not. Clara certainly did not. FBI documents show that in short order, the secretaries were jostling among themselves and challenging Clara's husband as to who would be #1 with him.

After numerous catastrophes and mass exodus from the Nation of Islam, the Honorable Elijah Muhammad began to handle his domestic circumstances better, and the women and their children lived well. They drove Jaguars, Mercedes, and other expensive cars and were given houses and apartments. They were paid generous allowances, tax-free, delivered personally by the Supreme Captain, the FOI Captain, the chief investigator, or another close confidant of Clara's husband. Elijah Muhammad, Jr. said, *"I personally would deliver money to the women."*[159]

It was reported but unconfirmed that rings were given to some women in some instances and that private ceremonies conducted outside of public view. However, the secretaries' public designation as wives was only made decades later – 1993 – by Minister Louis Farrakhan, not by the Honorable Elijah Muhammad while he was alive and not while Clara was alive. Some accepted the public gathering and introductions by Minister Louis Farrakhan as dignified protection for the women and their children. Others saw it as theatrics and held on to the searing memories of how the women treated Clara while she was alive. On the stage under the spotlight, the former secretaries' articulations as mature women in 1993 reflected considerable amnesia of their behavior in the 1960s.

Clara's husband made statements to the family such as, "*My wife is dead to me,* and *I need new children who have no bad feelings against me.*" One female close to the family said that Clara's conclusion was that how her husband executed his behavior had been incited by the lowest common denominator, not the highest. Nathaniel Muhammad reported, "*My father became dissatisfied with his eight children who, as they grew in knowledge, defied his authoritative leadership and his interpretation of Master Fard Muhammad as G-D. He said he wanted new children who were not corrupted.*"[160] Elijah Muhammad, Jr. disagreed and reported a different story: "*My father never threw us [eight children] away. He did want more children and told us and their mothers to make certain they go to school and get educated. My father did look at the life of Prophet Muhammad, PPBUH, and that's where he went off. He regretted his decisions. He told all of us he regretted his decisions. I was at the table when he told the secretaries, and all of them were present, he said, '...and all of you together cannot equal Clara.'*"[161]

Clara's silent suffering continued. She became territorial, emotionally sensitive, standing her ground in spaces in her home, fighting for her dignity. When the news about her husband became public, the membership of the Nation of Islam responded in shock, disgust, and disbelief. Elijah scolded ministers for not providing sufficient shield for his actions. Eventually, the suggestions of Malcolm X – recommending scriptural prerogatives as a justification – were accepted and used by Elijah and some ministers. Nevertheless, Malcolm and Wallace were accused of slandering the Nation of Islam leader. Some ministers said nothing. Eventually, Clara's husband gave her a rationale for his actions, citing the Bible and Qur'an as his support.

For Clara, the explanations were not sufficient, and daily catty slights from secretaries in her own home made her life miserable. Nevertheless, she silently suffered for the greater mission of the Honorable Elijah Muhammad. One secretary felt particularly emboldened and initiated a verbal confrontation with Clara in the presence of others in her home. The young woman said she was the *First Lady of the Nation of Islam*. It was an ugly exchange recalled by witnesses as totally disrespectful to Clara. Elijah Muhammad, Jr., said he spoke to his father about the incident, insisting that no one disrespected his mother, Clara Muhammad. It was reported that Clara put the young woman in her place with grace and dignity but firm resolve. The secretary reported the incident to Elijah, and his response was shocking.

Elijah Muhammad put Clara Muhammad out of the Nation of Islam. Her grandson, Herbert (Jesus) Muhammad, Jr., confirmed, *"Grandmother got 30 days in Class C because she was arguing at the table in front of guests openly disagreeing with the Honorable Elijah Muhammad."*[162] Another family member who lived in the mansion reported that Elijah's response was because of her arguments and resistance to his conduct with the secretaries. Minister Louis Farrakhan reported, *"Sister Clara Muhammad told me there was one part of the Holy Qur'an she hated, and that was the part that allowed a man more than one wife. The Honorable Elijah Muhammad [later] asked her, 'Do you mean to say that you hate what Allah has written in this book – Holy Qur'an?'"*[163]

In late 1962, Clara was forbidden to attend any Mosque or University of Islam. She could not have contact with any Muslim members except her family. When guests arrived at the mansion, Clara was forbidden to greet them or sit at the table. The secretaries welcomed all guests and sat at the table. The cooks could not cook for Clara; she had to prepare her own meals. She had her meals in the small breakfast nook off the kitchen. It was reported Clara was furious but maintained her dignity. She continued to care for her husband, nursing his bronchial asthma and other ailments if needed. When she cooked her own food, she would prepare enough for him, and he ate it. One family member reported, *"I never witnessed such cruelty on his part and such dignity and strength on hers. She was so* strong."[164] It was reported Clara said, *"How could he put me out when I brought him to the Saviour and was a builder of this Nation?"* Her children were outraged and came to her aid. The daughters, in particular, criticized their father for her and wanted her to leave him. They collectively assured her she would be taken care of. Family members reported she was extremely unhappy but made herself busy transferring her anger and pain into loving acts for her children and grandchildren.

Clara had frequently taken short trips to get away from the stress of her marital issues but always returned. This, however, was the breaking point. She decided to leave Elijah. She called Akbar and said she wanted to return to Egypt. In June of 1963, Clara took a plane to Cairo, Egypt, alone and distraught. The flight from Chicago to Cairo was time for Clara to contemplate. She may indeed have made the statement about hating the provision of polygyny in The Qur'an, and countless women have responded similarly. Young women, first time married who grew up with fanciful notions about love and marriage, often were the most opposed. Others across all age groups frequently believed a man having an affair was easier for them to accept than his marrying more than one woman. Although a historical practice throughout civilization, polygyny was a foreign concept to the new Muslims and not readily accepted. Over time, believing women have come to respect the provision of polygyny, which simply required increased knowledge and understanding and appropriate application on the part of the man.

The Chapter in The Qur'an titled The Women (Al Nissa, 4:3) says a man may take up to four wives if he treats them equally. Equal treatment is stressed because Allah, The Creator, says a man has one heart, and his one heart will always favor one woman above the rest. Therefore, equal treatment compensates for unequal feelings. The life of Prophet Muhammad ibn Abdullah, PPBUH, to whom The Qur'an was revealed, is especially important here because he provides a model of how Islamic life, including polygyny, is to be practiced. However, due to his prophetic status, Prophet Muhammad, PPBUH, was afforded rights and privileges above the average Muslim in the number of wives he was permitted.

One of the most authentic sources says, "The Messenger of Allah, PPBUH, had nine wives in wedlock...but...married thirteen women."[165] Two wives were immediately given back to their families, and two women were concubines. Therefore, most sources report he had nine or eleven wives. Prophet Muhammad ibn Abdullah, PPBUH, was married to one woman, his first wife, Khadijah bint Khuwaylid for 25 years. She was fifteen years his senior, wealthy and proposed marriage to him. When she passed away, he was 50 years old; only then did he marry other women. The second marriage was to a widow nearly 55 years old with five children whose husband had been killed in battle defending Al-Islam. He felt obligated to provide for them. She wanted to marry him to assist him in his prophetic mission by caring for his children, who now had no mother.[166] Some sources say the marriage was not sexually consummated as the woman only wanted the protection of the Prophet.

Scholars agree that the majority of the women the Prophet married were old, divorced, deserted, or captives from wars. The objective of the Prophet, PPBUH, was to provide and protect women and children, build alliances, and unite tribes to establish Al-Islam on the Arabian Peninsula. Aware of their age and circumstances, these women also frequently relinquished their personal time with the Prophet to enable him to be with the one he chose to marry as an intimate wife. Aisha bint Abu Bakr, daughter of Abu Bakr, was the only virgin woman Prophet Muhammad married, PPBUH.[167] He did conceive a child with Safiyyah, named Ibrahim, who died in infancy.

Although loved and revered, the Honorable Elijah Muhammad did not attain a status not comparable to that of Prophet Muhammad ibn Abdullah, PPBUH. Elijah Muhammad's decisions regarding his domestic life were not divine injunctions to advance the Nation as some continue to promote. There was never a discussion or directive from W. D. Fard

Muhammad that Elijah Muhammad make such decisions. They were his personal choices with searing lessons to learn if one would heed. The Honorable Elijah Muhammad may well have wanted his biological seed to multiply, but Allah, The Almighty, wants the seeds of faith to multiply. That was the prayer of Prophet Abraham (Ibrahim) stated in The Qur'an in the second Chapter of Al Baqarah, (The Cow/ Heifer) 2:128:

"Our Lord! make of us Muslims, bowing to Your Will, and of our progeny, a community of Muslims, bowing to Your Will; And show us our place for the celebration of (due) rites, and turn unto us (in Mercy); for You are the Oft-Returning, Most Merciful."

Biological seeds may or may not come into the faith, but spiritual seeds will advance the plan of Allah, The Most High. The Honorable Elijah Muhammad said, "My job was to clean you up. The one to come after me will bring a new religion." "There will be no successor…G-D chose me, and if He wants a successor, He will choose one." Meaning no one could take Elijah's place; he was singular, unique, and his phase of the work of raising his people was completed. Did he groom his son Wallace for the position? No, he was not qualified to groom Wallace to bring the new religion. Wallace was groomed by Allah through his dedicated study of The Qur'an and his refusal to acknowledge any G-D but Allah. Although he had issues with his son, Elijah believed in the word of W. D. Fard Muhammad, who designated to him and Clara that Wallace was the *heir apparent and would help both Fard and Elijah advance their work.*

While some prefer to hold on to unsubstantiated quibbles denying Wallace as the *heir apparent,* Imam W. Deen Mohammed publicly announced, *"I asked my father years before he passed, 'Daddy is there anything you need to tell me that I need to know?' My father dropped his head for a moment then raised it again and said to me, 'Son, it's best that the man going out don't interfere with the man coming in.'"*

On December 13, 1977, the heir apparent Wallace, as

the new leader of the Nation of Islam, addressed the Muslim community at a community night lecture in Chicago attended by more than 600 people. He titled his talk, *The Honorable Elijah Muhammad and the Dishonorable Elijah Muhammad.* The title and subsequent lecture garnered the ire of some of his father's devoted followers and some family members. However, his comments had already been confirmed by his father's behavior and recorded by the FBI. Wallace (Imam W. Deen Mohammed) stated he wanted to publicize the issues because others were preparing to profit from them by publishing scandalous books, movies, and tabloids. He further told the group of Muslims why certain aspects of the Nation of Islam had to evolve to be consistent with The Qur'an if a people were to have a dignified future as intelligent and moral human beings. He reviewed the outstanding contributions of his father but also his human failings and said, *"That which is consistent with The Qur'an we will keep, and that which is not we will let go."*[168]

CHAPTER 12: CLARA IN EGYPT

Cairo was a booming international city in 1963, with Cairo International Airport being the busiest airport in Africa. Gamal Abdel Nasser was the president of the legendary country of pyramids and political challenges. Akbar Muhammad, the youngest son of Clara and Elijah, attended Al Azhar University, the coveted Islamic University. He was fulfilling his goal to be the first in the Nation of Islam with a Ph.D.

Akbar and his bride Harriet welcomed Clara with open arms. Being with them was a safe harbor for her. Harriet said, *"Clara had been living in a bubble, doing everything for the family and the Nation. With little resources in the early days, she did not spend on herself. When things got financially better she could not venture out of the house by herself for security reasons. To have someone take her to downtown Chicago, particularly Marshall Field, was practically all she could do."*[169]

Harriet was best friends with Ethel and Lottie Rayya and previously worked as a secretary for Clara's husband. She also wrote a column in *Muhammad Speaks* newspaper. Harriet was very close to the Honorable Elijah Muhammad, who commissioned her to establish a bank for the Nation of Islam. She was very familiar with the family and worked in several businesses before she came into the Nation of Islam. Clara approved of her marriage to Akbar, and they shared mother/daughter affection.

Upon reflection, Harriet said, *"Over the years, I had occasion to observe Clara's behavior. She was such a warm, quiet person who never thought much of the limelight. She was not interested in being in the public. She was on the quiet side, but she could talk. She observed everything. She was not a wilting lily. When Clara wanted to speak her mind, she did just that. You always knew where you were with Clara Muhammad. She was firm but gentle at the same time. If she liked you, you would know it. If she didn't, you could feel it.*[170]

"She had plenty of money [in later years], but she would not waste anything. She would wash her stockings out every night and wear that single pair until they had a run (tear). Only then would she discard them and wear a new pair. In Chicago, when we would go shopping, we would go to Marshall Field a lot. And they knew her. There was one white woman who would always wait on her. In the dressing room between changes, the woman saw Clara's legs, and the woman gasped and said, 'Oh, Mrs. Muhammad, you have beautiful legs.' Clara thanked her and looked puzzled. The woman then said, 'I thought you were deformed. I thought that was why you wore long dresses.'"[171]

The experience of Clara in Egypt could not have been possible without her daughter-in-law Harriet Muhammad, as her son Akbar was in school and working. Following is Harriet's narration of the experience: *"I vividly recall Clara's arrival. She was in pain, very unhappy about her domestic situation. When she came to Cairo is when I got to know her best. It was the first time in her life that she got to relax and just enjoy things. She lived in the apartment with Akbar and me, she had the guest room. We just did everything together. She was my little traveling buddy. We were like two girls out on the town. We went to the movies; remember, back home in the Nation of Islam, we did not go to the movies. In Egypt, they had all of the latest American movies. In the afternoons we went to the movies. It was a real treat for her. I think she may have never gone to a movie. We went to several operas. One, in particular, was the famous Egyptian singer at the time, Umm Kulthum. We saw her in person. She loved Umm Kulthum. We didn't know a word she was saying, but it was wonderful.*

"We would get into a taxi; we could barely count our money. We would keep a card from the hotel where we lived and have them take us to the shopping area. We would then get out of the cab and walk to the shops, buying little trinkets and souvenirs. We would walk until we were worn out. Then we would hail a taxi, give

our address and go back to the hotel. I did not observe any health problems from Clara. She appeared very healthy and kept up with me with all the walking and everything.

"We would go to ice cream parlors, we took boat rides up the Nile. While Akbar and I were there, we were acting as attaché for the Nation of Islam. So we were invited to most of the embassy parties that were given around the city. Clara had a chance to go with us to those parties. She just loved it. We went to the Pyramids of Giza and Abu Simbel; at Luxor, the Valley of the Kings. And we went to Kenya, the three of us, and visited a Maasai village at Maasai Mara National Park. That was an adventure. The Maasai men wore only a little orange loincloth. They were standing around looking at us like we were special, and we were looking at them like they were special. So a breeze would come by and blow up the loincloths, and all of their genitals would be exposed. Clara just about died. She had a conniption fit. She said, Oh my G-D, Oh my G-D, Oh no! I don't want to see that! It happened throughout the day."

The motherly instincts of Clara were visible during their trip to Kenya: *"The children she saw disturbed her. A great number of them had eye infections, and the flies would connect to the pus around their eyes. The infections were so bad and appeared so common the children didn't even flutter the flies away. They just let them sit there. And Clara is looking at this and feeling all kinds of emotions about those poor children. She commented, 'Why don't they bat the flies away? Shoo them away or something?' Do something, you know. They didn't, and that bothered her. She didn't like looking at the children.*

"They gave us special treatment because we were escorted around the village by the Chief. He invited all three of us into his hut. Clara refused to come into his hut. It was a dung hut made of cow dung, and it was very low. You had to bend over to enter it. Once you entered, you walked through hallways to get to the main room. It was big enough to seat perhaps twenty people. Clara refused to come in; she just stood outside all the time we were in the hut. When we came out, she was almost in tears. She said, 'This is terrible. This is as bad as it gets.' She was very emotional about the whole scene. She

saw deprivation and poverty, and it affected her. It really bothered her. So in sum, her trip to the Maasai village was not as exciting as the one to Egypt, but she liked Nairobi. We stayed at the New Stanley Hotel there. The food was delicious. She ordered roast gilt, which was a small chicken-like bird, a special delicacy. One of the desserts she loved had fresh strawberries and real cream. It was a very rich creamy cream that was cream colored, not white, and the most delicious strawberries I have ever tasted. Even today, years later, I remember that taste. We visited a coffee plantation and picked green beans. She enjoyed that. We stayed in Kenya for a little over a week.

"As we returned to Egypt, I was unable to enter the country due to the fact that I did not have the proper immunization shots when I first entered the country, something I thought was in order. That was stunning to me. Akbar and Clara went back to Cairo, and I was quarantined for two weeks. The barrack-like facility had no bedding on the cots and the worst food or no food. Clara cooked for me every day, and Akbar brought the food and linen. I was finally released and reunited with them.

"To me, Clara Muhammad was an example of how to persevere in hard times; how to be strong. She was a loyal wife and mother, a gentle but powerful, beautiful woman. She was my mother-in-law, my travel buddy, and my friend, and I loved her."[172]

CHAPTER 13: THE MISSION IS GREATER

On October 17, 1963, Clara returned to Chicago with Akbar and Harriet. Although Akbar had encouraged her to stay with his father, it is believed she made up her own mind shortly after she left Chicago. The decision was strongly influenced by her promise to W. D. Fard Muhammad. He knew Elijah would need the support she provided, which is why the position of this author is that W. D. Fard Muhammad chose the pair as builders of *The Lost Found Nation of Islam in the Wilderness of North America.*

Clara said to many, including Minister Louis Farrakhan, *"In the forty (40) years I followed Master Fard Muhammad, I know of nothing I have done that would make me ashamed to stand before Allah."* No one else can testify to anything Clara Muhammad did that was against the laws of the Nation of Islam or Al-Islam. No one in the general membership, male or female, or in the hierarchy of the Nation of Islam made negative statements about her – not John Ali, Jeremiah Shabazz, Supreme Captain Raymond Sharrieff or any Captain of the women. No one publically said anything disparaging about Clara Muhammad except one person – Minister Louis Farrakhan.

Beginning in the late 1970s, Clara was accused of being the reason why her son transitioned to the Nation of Islam – to punish his father for hurting his mother. Throughout the 1980s, members of Minister Farrakhan's Nation of Islam were actually taught via their Self Improvement Study Guides that Clara was responsible for her illness and death due to her diminished faith in the "divine injunctions" of Elijah Muhammad to have additional wives and children. In a letter dated March 29, 1991, Minister Farrakhan said to his membership her emotional immaturity contributed to Clara's lack of faith in W.D. Fard Muhammad and Elijah Muhammad and resulted in her illness and subsequent death. This is a decades old narrative which continues to be taught, that the faith of Clara Muhammad was weakened because she did not see the divine injunctions in her husband's behavior but rather experienced emotional pain and illness as a result of it.

What Clara Muhammad was experiencing was a test of faith instructive to women everywhere. Every human being has something or someone they potentially cling to or regard as exalted. As a result of her love and unwavering commitment to her husband, Clara began to realize the higher lesson she was being tested to learn: *La Ilaha Illallah Muhammadan Rasoullulah* – There is no G-D but Allah, and Muhammad ibn Abdullah is the Messenger of Allah. Her test is the test every human being must answer in one's lifetime consistent with the *Covenant* created in the *fitra* (human nature) at birth.[173]

If one worships a person or thing other than the One G-D, one will have to face that reality before one leaves this earth. This is not an issue of how Clara handled her emotions or whether her faith diminished faith after she became ill from the trauma of what she was witnessing by her husband. If the behavior of her husband could bring down a Nation, it certainly could bring down a woman, and it did, thousands of them. The issue is not emotions; the issue is truth, honesty, and reality. Clara Muhammad went through a period of grief, but her faith was strengthened because of her honesty and purity. She had no diminished faith. Clara came into reality, into a clear, rational understanding of W. D. Fard Muhammad and Elijah Muhammad. She was permitted to see that there is no G-D but Allah, The Most High. Clara would often say, *Every tub must stand on its own bottom.* Her test now was to live her life still supporting the best of her husband but standing on her own [spiritual] bottom. As every human being comes into this world naked and alone, one will leave this world naked and alone.

Clara Muhammad resolved that the mission was greater, that Allah was Greater, than anyone or anything. She kept her promise to W. D. Fard Muhammad and supported Elijah regardless. And she raised Wallace. It was still challenging for her, but Clara would not relent. She resolved to support the Honorable Elijah Muhammad and the Nation of Islam until her last breath, and she did. With a renewed spirit, Clara decided she would continue the marriage and support the Honorable Elijah Muhammad but would also live the best life she could for herself. She was eager to see her family and was ready for the next chapter of her life.

Upon her arrival home, Elijah was of a different mindset. He was more respectful and appeared stunned that she had left and stayed away as long as she did. He offered his *mea culpa* in his own way but was enmeshed in the consequences of his decision to father children with his secretaries. That decision breached the Nation of Islam, and the fallout was being felt inside and outside the community.

Earlier in the year, on January 1, 1963, Elijah Jr. picked up Wallace from prison and provided details about the status of his mother, father, and the Nation. Wallace knew some of what was transpiring via family correspondence but was more livid about the pain and humiliation his mother was encountering. Being with her proved to be mutually comforting.

In April 1963, Malcolm met with the Honorable Elijah Muhammad to discuss the matter of his domestic circumstances and offer his solutions. By the end of the year, the indiscretions of the Honorable Elijah Muhammad permeated the public. The assassination of President John F. Kennedy in November 1963 and the remarks of Malcolm X ("The chickens have come home to roost") also put the Nation of Islam and Malcolm X in the spotlight. It appeared that whatever Malcolm did or said would be used against him by the three known forces at work seeking to destroy the Nation of Islam: 1) the FBI, 2) those personally seeking to destroy Malcolm, and 3) those seeking to derail Wallace as *heir apparent.*

By June 1964, Malcolm became the lightning rod for the disclosures about the Honorable Elijah Muhammad's personal life; Wallace was put out of the Nation for perceived culpability; Akbar left on his own, based on ideology (he would make a public statement by December 1964), and the FBI pushed in further, using its disruptive tactics to destroy the Nation.

Although his father was inspired by what Wallace taught from The Qur'an, the rationale for his expulsion was that he was not teaching what the Nation stood on – that W. D. Fard Muhammad was G-D and Elijah Muhammad was the messenger. Decades later, in the 1980s, Wallace (Imam W. Deen Mohammed) described the incident: *"I stood at the door (4847 S. Woodlawn Avenue) with my mother. She was in great pain and did not want me to leave. She said to me, 'Just go in there and tell your father what he wants to hear.' I said to her, 'Mama, I can't do that. Did he [W. D. Fard Muhammad] ever tell you he was G-D?' She hesitated for a moment and said, 'Well, son, no. He said don't even call him prophet. He said prophet was too big a name for him.' So I said, 'Mama, a man who would tell you Prophet is too big a name for him, how could you now want me to call him G-D?'"*[174]

Wallace did not tell his father W. D. Fard Muhammad was G-D. He never taught that W. D. Fard Muhammad was G-D, and with his mother in tears, he was put out of the Nation of Islam from 1964 to 1965 before his father permitted his return. For the sake of unity, he returned after Malcolm was assassinated and made a public appearance and apology at the Saviour's Day Convention in 1965. His following statement in the 2003 documentary, *"This Far By Faith,"* explains: *"Well, the Nation of Islam was precious to us as a means of moving us from the old Negro, the old Black man, to the new Black man. So, to save the child for the future was what I had on my mind. And to defeat whatever the enemies of the Nation of Islam were doing to divide the leadership and disillusion the followers. That is all I was responding to: The Nation of Islam at risk; the Honorable Elijah Muhammad needs help in this serious time."*[175]

He further said, *"I loved the Nation of Islam...I saw it*

prodding us on to our destiny where we would see our true human value better. But I also heard it whispering to us, 'You don't have it yet quite right.'" And what the Nation did not have quiet right was the correct concept of G-D.

Clara's son said when he was a child of thirteen, he was left at home alone and was frightened by the squeaks and noises of a wood-framed house. He then prayed to G-D the following prayer, *"Oh Allah, if I am not seeing you correctly, will you please help me see you correctly."* He continued, *"What was bothering me...was the logic. I was told white people are devils and...I see this picture of the man who taught my father and gave my father his mission...his name was Fard, we called him the Saviour...and I am not comfortable with that picture [of a white man as G-D]. As I got older and braver to face things that were not settling with me too well – ideas about the origin of man and G-D... it took me from the Nation of Islam teachings...I was changing the way I thought and the way I perceived reality."*

On another occasion, he said, *"I asked my father, Daddy is there anything you need to tell me that I need to know? My father dropped his head for a moment. When he raised it he said, "Son, it's best that the man going out does not interfere with the man coming in."* Imam Mohammed said he knew years before his father passed what changes the Nation of Islam needed to get it on the right path to authentic human freedom. And that path began with: 1) the correct concept of G-D, 2) human identity (male and female), and 3) the correct understanding of scripture.

When he was the last put out of the Nation of Islam (1964-1965), those who felt he betrayed the Honorable Elijah Muhammad theologically and personally spoke ill of him, intimidated him, hunted him down, and tried by the end of the year to kill him. Clara stepped in and told Elijah, *"You better not hurt a hair on his head."*[176] Elijah himself reported on a radio broadcast, *"Do not touch my son Wallace or grandson Hasan. Allah will take care of them."* Grandson Hasan Sharif says, *"My grandfather would not hurt Uncle Wallace or myself. If that thinking was out there, it was coming from others. He would not do that, and he did not order Malcolm to be killed."*

It is believed that when Clara returned from Egypt, she became aware that her role as Mother of the Nation was more significant than she imagined. She was the initial link that connected a people to their lost Islamic heritage through W. D. Fard Muhammad. She knew her son Wallace, named after him, was destined to be the new leader. But after nearly 40 years of observing firsthand the Nation of Islam, Clara came to realize that the help Wallace would provide was not what she initially thought.

More than anyone, Clara supported the Honorable Elijah Muhammad and was intensely aware of the human failings of the man. She observed in the early 1930s how Elijah deified W. D. Fard Muhammad when Fard did not teach anyone he was G-D. That was the point of conflicting departure of the early Muslims during the establishment of the *Lost Found Nation of Islam.* She was devastated by her husband's indiscretions with women and aggression towards Wallace. The assassination of Malcolm X on February 21, 1965, was painful, although she did not believe her husband was responsible. Clara was also aware of the increased moral corruption, mishandling of resources, and self-promotion among ministers over Temples that began in the mid-1960s, at the expense of the ordinary Believers. Her role now as *Mother of the Nation* was to ensure that Wallace took the Nation of Islam forward – to The Qur'an – signified by her words and the last gift she gave him as she was terminating.

Elijah had already set the stage for The Qur'an as the guide; he carried it everywhere, read it, referred to it, and quoted it. W. D. Fard Muhammad gave him a copy of it in the language it was revealed – Arabic – and told him to learn Arabic. In his soon-to-be-published book, *Message to the Blackman in America,* Elijah even included a guide to understanding The Qur'an and the Bible. However, without the facility of the Arabic language, his understanding of The Qur'an was minimal. Elijah realized that fact and made teaching Arabic in the University of Islam schools, and having his two youngest sons learn it, essential. Clara would honor her promise to W. D. Fard Muhammad and support her husband as long as she lived, but she would also protect her son Wallace to enable him to further the work he was destined to do. It was a delicate balance she had to maintain.

Clara brought her brother Carlton to live with her in 1967 since he was ill. He later lived with Nathaniel and was eventually moved to a nursing home, where he died in September 1974. Her father, Quartus, joined her in 1964. He loved his daughter, and his presence in the home was healing for her. Quartus became a Muslim and attended Temple #2. It is reported he said, *He could not have imagined that the poor Elijah Poole whom he threatened with a shotgun to stay away from his daughter was now the Honorable Elijah Muhammad.*

Nathaniel Muhammad reported, *"My grandfather was a dignified man. He attended the Mosque and was registered as a Muslim – Quartus X."*[177] He and his youngest daughter, Rose Ameenah, eventually returned to Atlanta, Georgia, where they both passed. Quartus passed July 25, 1965, was buried at South-View Cemetery, Atlanta, and Rose Ameenah signed his death certificate. She married, had two other children, and died on October 4, 1989. It is unclear if Quartus knew the particulars of his daughter's marital strife.

The following headstone was placed on the previously unmarked grave of Quartus X Evans by Nasir Muhammad, founder of Black Mecca Tours, Atlanta, Georgia. Bro. Nasir worked diligently to secure funds so that the father of Clara, and father-in-law of Elijah Muhammad, would be buried with dignity. Quartus Evans is buried at the historic South-View Cemetery in Atlanta, Georgia. It is also the final resting place of the Honorable AME Bishop Henry McNeal Turner, Atlanta's first Black millionaire; Alonzo F. Herndon of Atlanta Life Insurance; Rev. A. D. Williams, grandfather of Rev. Dr. Martin Luther King, Jr.; Reverend & Mrs. Martin Luther King, Sr.; Ruby Doris Smith-Robinson of Student Nonviolent Coordinating Committee (SNCC); John Wesley Hobbs, grandfather of Atlanta's first Black mayor; Maynard Jackson; Representative Julian Bond, NAACP and SNCC member; Mattiwilda Dobbs, famous opera singer; National Basketball Association (NBA) Hall of Fame athlete Walt Bellamy, and many more who paved the way for current and future generations.

During a period when Clara appeared to be unwell and needed reassurance, she asked her daughter Lottie Rayya, *"Do you think I did a good job with my children?"* Lottie Rayya recalled she answered, *"Yes Mama, I think you did. We did alright. None of us had to go to jail (only when the boys went for not registering for the draft), no broken bones, no real illnesses, you did a really good job raising your children...You stood by my father, you held the Nation up all these years, you worked real hard. You fed the people by the thousands, you did that cooking and sweating over a hot stove for years, you did everything. You gave them everything. And so, she felt better about it."*[178]

"We continued to talk about the children how we all were working for the community in different ways; we all had positions one way or the other and then we got to my brother Wallace. Well, one thing about Wallace, she [Clara] said, 'I'm not worried about Wallace. He is going to be alright.'"[179]

The magnum opus, *Message to the Blackman in America*, was published by Elijah Muhammad in 1965. Admonishing and inspiring, it shocked America. The book did not include Clara by name or her contribution to the founding, building, or shaping of the Nation of Islam. The omission of her legacy is why Muslims were surprised when they learned that it was Clara who first encountered W. D. Fard Muhammad, took Elijah to meet him, and saved the Nation from collapse during Elijah's flights from adversaries and imprisonment.

Hosting Dr. MLK, Jr. and Wife and Civil Rights Leaders

A gentleman named John Ali came to the Nation with a unique skill set and was further groomed by the Honorable Elijah Muhammad from 1960 to 1970. He became the National

Secretary for the Nation of Islam, and when interviewed, he spoke of Clara Muhammad: *"She was kind, compassionate, and a great hostess. She and her husband treated everyone who came to their home with graciousness and hospitality."* The former National Assistant Secretary, Agieb Bilal, said of John Ali, *"He virtually single-handedly took the operations of protocol from a mom-and-pop enterprise to a dignified international office befitting a head of state. After all, it was the NATION of Islam. If a comparison must be made, his role would be equivalent to a White House chief of staff."*[180]

John Ali would go to the mansion daily and provide briefings on each dignitary scheduled to meet the Honorable Elijah Muhammad. Clara would sit in on many of those briefings and often ask questions. Anyone who wanted to meet with the Honorable Elijah Muhammad first came in contact with John Ali. That included Muslim diplomats and dignitaries from Muslim countries, Africa, the Caribbean, and the United States. *"I recall when Martin Luther King, Jr. arrived, each time,"* he said. *"Dr. King initiated the meetings and came with Ralph Abernathy, Andrew Young, and Stokely Carmichael, and a few others on one occasion."*

"They came in the morning and were first made comfortable and served coffee and tea. I remember Dr. King commenting, 'We are two boys from Georgia.'" It is frequently missed that the Honorable Elijah Muhammad and Dr. Martin Luther King, Jr. could converse on the Bible as each knew it well. John Ali continued, *"People were surprised to see the level of dignity and sophistication of the Muslims."* The perception prevaling though erroneous was that the Muslims were the underclass.

On the second occasion that Dr. King visited Clara's husband and brought Mrs. Coretta Scott King., as the two leaders conversed, Clara and Mrs. King sat together with the other guests and exchanged conversation over a meal. Requests to the King Center staff, and directly to Reverend Bernice King to review the diary/archives of Mrs. Coretta Scott King's meeting with Clara Muhammad, were to no avail. Referencing the photograph confirmed her presence at 4847 S. Woodland

Avenue, but no one at the King Center seemed aware of the meeting with Clara Muhammad. However, the women in the Muhammad household recalled it vividly.

Geneva Walker Muhammad, the wife of Clara's nephew Clarence, recalls, *"I was there when Dr. King and his wife came. She was so pretty. They were very warm and gracious. I was a cook and enjoyed every day of cooking; I cooked for everybody."* When asked if she served them? Geneva said, *"No! I prepared buffet style."*[181]

Halimah Muhammad-Ali, a granddaughter, started working in the mansion at 12 1/2 years old. He was fifteen when Dr. King and his wife visited. *"We had to leave school [University of Islam] early to prepare for their arrival. We had to pull out and polish all the silver. We prepared a rolling cart with tea, pure cream, condiments, coffee, brown sugar, and bottled water and rolled it into the living room. My grandfather was very excited. When they arrived, he said, 'Everyone, I want you to meet Dr. Reverend Martin Luther King, Jr.' Dr. King bowed his head and said, 'Good Evening.' My grandfather then said, 'Clara, I want you to take care of the dinner guests and escort Mrs. King to the table.' Grandmother and Mrs. King and a few other women and a few men assembled in the dining room. Grandfather and Dr. King closed the sliding doors to the massive living room and stayed in there from approximately 3 p.m. to sunset – the sun was going down. When they finally came out, I heard my grandfather say, 'Brother, I will get our people here, but I want you to go to the mountain top and shout it over there.' They were coming together."* [182]

Ruqaiyah Muhammad-Farrar recalled, *"I remember when John Ali briefed my grandparents on a potential visit from a Saudi prince. Grandmother asked him about the women in the country, their roles, and circumstances; she was well-informed. When the prince visited, she was able to engage him in conversation."* In each instance, Clara welcomed her guests with the highest social graces.

As Clara continued to do her work internally, the Nation of Islam struggled to maintain its moral standards and social influence. Testimonies of Muslim women's adoration and allegiance to her husband appeared in articles in the Nation's newspaper, *Muhammad Speaks*. Popular columns such as *The Woman in Islam* and others were written by secretaries of Elijah Muhammad. In 1967 Clara wrote her own article in *Muhammad Speaks* newspaper. It may have been an effort to reassert her value to the Nation. The article praised her husband and appealed to others to follow and support him. She in no way elevated herself, but she did note the hardships she and her children encountered to establish the Nation of Islam. The article was well-received by virtually all who read it. However, her granddaughter Halimah Muhammad-Ali reported, *"Grandfather did not like that she wrote the article. He told her not to write anymore, that this was his time."*[183]

Also, in 1967 Wallace made Hajj. His visit to the Ka'ba in Mecca, the first house established for the worship of One G-D by Prophet Adam and re-structured by Prophet Abraham/Ibrahim and his son Ishmael/Ismail, was another significant step in his Islamic development.

Clara continued to gather her children and grandchildren, celebrating the family and special events. She cooked her delicious food, gave her mother/grandmother advice, fed the needy, supported the sick, comforted and inspired the women. She continued to support education and the University of Islam. She had a comfort level in her nearly 70 years of life. She continued to receive guests at the mansion who visited her husband and excelled in her role as Mother of the Nation, hosting all who came to the mansion while teaching her granddaughters the special arts.

Clara and Elijah reached a rapprochement. She traveled with her husband, read, and kept up with world events. Her travels continued to enrich her views. She was able to see the impact of the Nation of Islam vis-à-vis global affairs, particularly evident in the political changes developing in African countries breaking from colonial rulers. She was intelligent, alert and well-informed, yet humble and unassuming. Those qualities seemed unappreciated by some who expected a woman in her position to be more ostentatious, bold, and self-absorbed. Still, the FBI had no limits and no moral compass. They were brutal in their tactics of intrusion. Clara did not accept her husband's extramarital behavior, and the women continued to pester her for recognition, requesting that she see their children. When things got difficult, she would travel to Florida to visit her brother or Lana Shabazz.

Saviour's Day 1970 found America in turmoil. It was a time of division between citizens and government over increased military aggression in Vietnam, the draft of primarily the poor and Black men, and the consequences of hundreds of years of crimes against Black people. The Civil Rights Act of 1964 and subsequent affirmative action[184] efforts demonstrated some government contrition. Yet, the continued assassination of people and programs seemed endless, be they presidents – John F. Kennedy; religious leaders – Martin Luther King, Jr.; or revolutionaries – Malcolm X and the Black Panther Party. The increased attendance at the annual Nation of Islam Saviour's Day signified that Black people were seeking a different path to freedom.

Between 1970 and 1971, a delegation of ministers, captains, and others brought a tape to Elijah Muhammad of Wallace (Imam W. Deen Mohammed) teaching at Temple #12 in Philadelphia. The significance was the tape revealed that Wallace taught *the problem for humanity was the misrepresentation of religion and the wrong understanding of scripture.* He said *The Qur'an was revealed to bring correction.* After listening to the tape, Elijah – although not in the best of health – jumped up from his seat at the dining room table of his mansion and said enthusiastically, "*My boy's got it. He can take that message anywhere. Clara, isn't this what we were waiting for? Clara nodded her head and said, 'Yes, thank Allah.'*"

CHAPTER 14: THE LAST DAYS

Approaching her seventy-third year, Clara was visiting Lana Shabazz in Florida. When interviewed, Minister Louis Farrakhan said, "*I was speaking at the University of Florida, and I knew that Mother was there, so I ordered bird of paradise flowers and brought them to Lana's house. She [Mother Clara] came out of the back ...where she was and said words to me, some of which I will not repeat. Then she asked me to describe the Palace that was being built [in Chicago]. I had just come from Chicago and gave her a description of the Palace, and she looked at me and said, 'I don't think I will live to see it.' That same year, she was in Mercy Hospital dying.*"[185] Clara had a sharp tongue for many of the ministers of Elijah Muhammad who sought to shield and dignify what she believed was his perfidious behavior.

Shakeelah Hasan reported, "*She called me [from Florida] and said she was not feeling well and not breathing well. I was alarmed and told her to come back to Chicago and see her doctor and get an x-ray.*"[186] Clara came back home and was hospitalized at Mercy Hospital the first week in July 1972. She was diagnosed with terminal inoperable stomach cancer. Nathaniel Muhammad said, "*She kept her illness to herself; she did not tell us. My father told us when it was terminal.*"[187]

A host of women, ministers, students, dignitaries, and Muslims in general sought to see her. Only her condition prevented many from expressing in person their love and appreciation for what she did for Al-Islam in America, for women, education, and the Nation of Islam. Prayers from Believers in Mosques around the country were offered for Clara. Students and teachers from the Universities of Islam sent scores of cards, letters, and flowers. Accompanied by Clark X (Muhammad Siddiq), Director of the University of Islam, New

York, Minister Farrakhan said, *"When I visited her at the hospital, her words to me were: 'Dear brother, I want you to help my husband. He is getting old now, and he can't do the things he used to do. I want you to help my husband.' Tears came from her eyes, and I wiped her tears and promised her that I would help her husband. That was the last time I saw my spiritual Mother alive."*[188]

Hafeesha Al Uqdah came into the Nation of Islam in Los Angeles, 1961. She and her husband, Jessie, were known for their charitable works despite her husband having only one leg. Their daughter Priscilla, a military veteran and alum of the University of Islam, championed the cause of Muslim schools among alumni. She founded the University of Islam and Clara Muhammad Schools National Alumni Association (1992) and for decades has worked to keep the vision of independent self-affirming education alive. Mrs. Al Uqdah traveled from Los Angeles to Chicago to visit her in the hospital, accompanied by several women Clara knew from the early days of the Nation of Islam. She said, *"Sister Clara was quiet, a very reserved person. However, if she knew you, she was very humorous and loved talking about her husband. But she was a very strong woman, and all of the things she and the sisters did establishing and supporting that school were the most memorable. Those days were the most beautiful days (the early days of the Nation of Islam)."*[189]

Mrs. Al Uqdah continued, *"We stayed about an hour and a half. Sister Clara was very sick, but she was laughing and in good spirits. She told us that her husband kept talking about the new home they were building in Arizona. She so thoroughly believed in the Honorable Elijah Muhammad and W. D. Fard Muhammad."* She said, *"Sister Clara said, 'They were building a new house in Arizona because of the need to be in another climate.' That she and Elijah both needed dry heat. It was just too cold and moist in Chicago for them. Sister Clara said, laughing, 'Elijah has just been talking about when his house is finished he will add this to it, and when he moves in, he is going to buy this and that'. Clara reportedly commented to him, 'Elijah, what are you talking about saying your house?' He said, 'Huh, don't worry about that, Clara. 'Anything that's mine is yours.*

It's your house too,' he said. Clara is reported to have responded, 'Yes, that's right, we both will be moving into that house.' She liked Arizona and was tired of the cold weather in Chicago."[190]

Elizabeth Shabazz left Philadelphia to visit Clara in the hospital. She said, "Mother Clara said to me, 'Girl, if Allah will bless me to get out of this bed, I am going to come visit you and go on with my life.'"[191] Hasan Sharif recalled, "Grandmother was in Mercy Hospital, sick, and I was out of the community along with Uncle Wallace. When I went to see her, I said 'As-Salaamu-Alaikum Grandmother,' and she said, 'Grandmother? You don't look like no grandson of mine with all that hair on your head, and you haven't had a shave.' I was shocked because she was sick! Being out of the community, I was wearing a natural dashiki and African beads around my neck and did not look like an FOI. Two days later, I went back to the hospital. I had a haircut, real short (I hated doing it), but I did it for her. I shaved, and I came back, and she smiled and said, 'Now you look like my grandson' and hugged me. She stood up for the program of the Honorable Elijah Muhammad all the way. She was a remarkable woman."[192]

Lottie Rayya recalled, "When my mother was sick, I didn't realize she was actually terminating. She met with her children, all of them. She wanted each one of us to do certain things. One by one, we came to visit and received instructions and gifts from her."[193] Imam W. Deen Mohammed said, "My mother only gave me religious items."[194]

Lottie Rayya continued, "She said to me, 'If Wallace would just make up with his father.' That was her desire. She wanted him to do that. So I went to him and said, 'I want Mama to die happy; I don't want her to be worried.' So he said, 'I'll talk to her.' He did talk to her, and I don't know what he said; she never told me. When he came out of the room, I was anxious. I asked what happened, 'What did you say?' He said, 'Oh, she's happy, she's happy.' That's all he said. You know how the Imam is, just a few words."[195]

Wallace was officially in Class F – put out of the Nation of Islam. Lottie Rayya continued, "I remember he would come to the hospital every day, sit on the floor outside of my mother's room and *read The Qur'an the entire time she was hospitalized [approximately three weeks]. She later told me, 'I am not worried about Wallace, He will be alright.'"* Clara knew what her son had to do and what she had prepared him to do. Lottie Rayya later reported, *"My mother told Wallace, 'Son, you go on and lead the people, they will follow you.' Then she gave him her final gift, her personal Qur'an."*[196]

Imam Mohammed later said, *"My honorable mother, Sister Clara Muhammad, before she expired only put into my possession religious items, no money, no jewelry, nothing of that nature. A postcard that she received in the mail after her delivery referring to me as Wallace D. Mohammed, and my mother also left to me her Qur'an. Two things, a postcard, and The Qur'an. In real measure, the role of The Qur'an in my life is not without Clara Muhammad's attendant influence. In that regard, my devotion to the Holy Book is of her legacy."*

Hasan Sharif said, *"I remember him saying she had given her Qur'an to him. He described it as, 'Small, could fit in the palm of your hand and was all in Arabic.' All four corners on the front and back were embedded with pearls. It had other colors and lots of gold running through it. It was delicate and beautiful."*[197]

Lottie Rayya said she continued to be distraught about her mother's sickness and turned to Wallace again. *"I don't know why I always turn right to him every time. I did know from a child that he would be the one that would take over when my father passed; I knew that. We all knew that almost before he was born because Master Fard made my father promise that, if he was a boy, to make him promise that he would help him with the mission. And my mother was always told to take special care of him. And she did; she took special care, although she beat the daylights out of him, she still took special care of him. She really did. So, I've always felt him to be close and thought him to be special. So I went to him and said, 'Can't we do something to help her because she was dying.' It looked like Allah would let her live; I really wanted him to pull some miracle for me. He came to me, and after he listened to what I had to say, he said, 'Well, we can only ask Allah just so many times. He saved her before.' Which He did, she had two surgeries before. He continued,*

'We can only ask Him to save her just so often.' He made me understand that The Qur'an says nothing happens without Allah's permission. I got comfort from that.[198]

"When I think about my mother, her main thing was the school. Graduation time, she loved it. She would get herself together and say, 'I've got to get money for the children. I'm' going to ask your father for some money...how do I look?' She made sure everything was just right. She never went out dirty, not one spot on herself. She was neat and clean at all times. And she would say, 'I'm going down and get some money in order to give it to the children.' She would give $5.00 to seniors and $3.00 to the eighth graders. And we had a big school, nearly 500 children. She loved graduation time. She would just sit there and admire the children when they would walk down the aisle. She would say, 'Don't they look pretty in their white dresses and their little suits.' She just loved it. And she would pass out roses to them on graduation day."[199]

Years later, discussing the legacy of his mother, Imam W. Deen Mohammed said, *"More important than the flowers or the money or gifts was that look on her face. I know my mother, I know that look of satisfaction and encouragement that she was pleased with me that said, 'Son, you made me so happy with you today. I am behind you to keep on doing what you are doing.' Her smile would light up her face, and she would look at you and make you feel so good and so rewarded for what you had done that she appreciated. And I saw her give that same look to the children who were not her children of her own blood. She would give them that same look; it was not in any way weaker than the look she gave to me. And I want the children of Sister Clara Muhammad School to know that. That Sister Clara Muhammad had the same interest in you all that she had in her own children. She had the same appreciation and happiness when she saw one of your children excelling that she had when she saw her own children excelling."*[200]

Clara decided she wanted to be home. The last week in July 1972, she was moved from the hospital to her bedroom with two capable nurses, Alberta Muhammad and Eloise Benita (Jameelah Muhammad), providing twenty-four-hour care. From that date until the 12th of August, family members continued to pour into the mansion to see her. Forgoing sound dietary advice to allow her to have whatever she wanted, her granddaughter Halimah Muhammad-Ali reported Clara requested a special meal of chicken wings and rice. She continued, *"I was in the room when two of the secretaries, Tynetta Muhammad and Lucille Muhammad, came into the bedroom with their then four (4) children. I remember Ishmael, in particular; he was the oldest. He saw my grandmother."*

Even in her most vulnerable state, Clara was gracious to her core and bore the situation with dignity. That was just the beginning of the secretaries' invasion of her personal space. In earlier conversations with her daughters, especially Ethel, Clara had expressed concerns about her jewelry. She did not want the secretaries to claim it and even suggested they bury the items with her. Within a few days, Clara went into a coma for an extended period, and each of the secretaries would come into her room to look at her. Never all at once, but each one took the opportunity, family members reported. In her intermittent consciousness, family said they could hear her recite, *The Lord is my shepherd, I shall not want.*

On August 6, 1972, the Honorable Elijah Muhammad published "The Theology Of Time" in *Muhammad Speaks* newspaper. It had the following introduction:

"I set up and laid around my poor wife suffering with pain and what not. I prayed over her. I don't care anything about too much sleep no way. God didn't make me to sleep very long. He told me and those others that were there listening to Him, 'He [Messenger] will be like myself, a couple of hours will be sufficient for him to sleep.' So, I sit up and laid around on the side of the bed honoring her in her helpless state of sickness. I noticed she would sleep sound as long as I was laying around on the bed or sitting there where she could open her eyes and see me. I hated to leave out for the sake of wanting to sleep and rest."

Granddaughter Halimah Muhammad-Ali said, *"Grandfather, fully dressed, laid on the bed next to Grandmother. He put his cheek next to hers and talked to her. Grandmother is in a coma but started moving her legs and body. Dr. Charles Willilams, Sr. of Chicago, the attendant physician, was present. He is reported to have said, 'You Muhammad people are so strange. I have never seen anyone in a coma move before.'"* Halimah Muhammad-Ali said, *"Later, I was in another part of the house, and something strong told me to go to Grandmother's room. When I arrived, her nurse, Sister Alberta Muhammad, was placing a resuscitator in her throat. I remember hearing water gurgle up, and then I heard her last breath."*

Nathaniel Muhammad said, *"At some point, we were all in the room with my mother, all of her children, Emmanuel, Ethel, Elijah, Jr., Lottie Rayya, Herbert, and Akbar, [Grandchildren] Ruqaiyah Muhammad and Halimah Muhammad, Hasan Sharif, and Elizabeth Shabazz, and Shakeelah Hassan were near the door in the hall. My father got in the bed with her. I was holding my mother's hand and heard her deeply exhale and believed that was her last breath. And I said to everyone, 'Mama's gone.'"* Shakeelah Hassan said, *"I was the one who pronounced her deceased and pulled the sheet over her face."*[201] Grandson Hasan Sharif said, *"I was in the room when she passed. I recall Dr. Charles Williams the doctor was in the room and had a stethoscope [around his neck], he pronounced my grandmother deceased."*

It was August 12, 1972. *"My grandfather was so grieved, my uncles had to hold him up to take him out of the room,"* reported Halimah Muhammad-Ali. One family member reported, *"He eventually returned with a prayer rug and made two rakah of prayer beside her bed."* Another said, *"No, I never saw him do that or prostrate in prayer."*

Hasan Sharif said, *"Uncle Wallace (who was put out of the Nation of Islam in Class F, which prohibited him from communicating with anyone) did not come into the house until after Grandmother passed. He came into the house and didn't say one word to anyone. He went straight to Grandmother's bed and made du'a (informal prayer). And as quickly as he came in, he turned around and left the house."* How he knew she had passed, no one knows.

Clara believed in the mission of her husband more than anyone alive. She witnessed the impact of "The Teachings" on Elijah and the people who followed him. Clara never moved into the new house in Arizona nor the big house, the Palace, in Chicago. But she kept her promise to Master W. D. Fard Muhammad – she supported her husband and raised her son, the next leader who would advance the Nation.

"My grandmother took a lot," said Ruqaiyah Muhammad-Farrar. *"I don't think any woman alive could have taken what she went through. She was a very strong woman who loved her family, loved the Nation, and to me, she was a martyr. I don't believe there's another one out there like her. And she always smiled, she was always pleasant and laughing, but she was hurting inside."*

Halima Muhammad-Ali, a granddaughter, said, *"My grandmother told me on her death bed, 'If someone does anything to you to upset you or bother you, tell them. If you don't, it will kill you just like it's killing me.'"* Although Clara eventually came into the knowledge that freed her soul, the many years of accepting behavior she knew was unacceptable had taken its toll. Ruqaiyah Muhammad-Farrar continued, *"The final gesture of disrespect was when my grandmother died, and they took her out of the mansion. The family, the cooks, the gardeners, the workers, everyone stood in honor of her. But not one of the secretaries stood for the First Lady of the Nation of Islam, not one. They disrespected her to the very end."*

Nathaniel Muhammad said, *"They took my mother's body from the house, and we followed in cars. It was a little after midday, nowhere near sunset. All of a sudden, a huge cloud came out of the sky and hung over the vehicle that carried her body. It was not a black cloud and not a white cloud, it was in between. It was huge but not scary [ominous]. When you see something in nature, even if you don't understand it, your soul registers a feeling that signals how you are to respond. It was not a feeling of doom or something negative. It was a feeling of awe, amazement, astonishment, and reverence. The cloud followed Mama's body to the mortuary and stayed in the sky until she was removed from the vehicle."* Hasan Sharif said, *"It then came down midway so that you had to turn on the headlights of your car to see the street, then it raised up and was gone."*

"My mother was a martyr," said Nathaniel Muhammad. *"I believe she went straight to Paradise/heaven. I was not the only one who saw what happened when they took her body out of the house. Everyone saw it."*

The Honorable Elijah Muhammad put a final notice in *Muhammad Speaks* newspaper, and the then-editor, Leon Forrest, and several Muslim women wrote beautiful tributes to Clara. A tribute from Marva Salimah Salaam, author of *Rose Against the Wind,*[202] and a dedicated teacher and member of the Nation of Islam, said: *"Sister Clara Muhammad possessed the poise and refinement of a queen. She had the courage to be different. She had the nerve and the pride to get out of the styles of short dresses and put on ankle-length ones, which she wore with great dignity. For those of us in the Nation of Islam, she was our first lady – feminine, firm, and faithful."*[203]

The Nation of Islam had not yet evolved into the fullness of Al-Islam. Therefore, the service for Clara was not an official *janaaza*. In that tradition, the deceased is washed in a specific manner and shrouded in two pieces of white cloth for females and three pieces for males. Viewing is in private for family and guests; for the public ceremony, the casket is closed. The burial may be with or without a casket, with the head facing the Ka'ba in Makkah. The Gilbert Mortuary prepared the body of Clara and said, *"She was prepared in the tradition of great ladies."*

The funeral for Clara Evans Muhammad drew a massive crowd, with estimates of more than 1,000 people. A morning service was held at Mosque #2, 7351 S. Stony Island Avenue, Chicago. The casket was open, and Clara was shrouded in soft pink, her favorite color. MGT and FOI poured in from around the country. They passed her coffin and saluted the Mother of the Nation. Minister James Shabazz officiated the services. At the end of the service, all were encouraged to eat a piece of peppermint candy, a tradition of the Nation of Islam signifying remembrance of the sweetness of life.

The Muhammad family sat in front row seats sectioned off by rope. The Honorable Elijah Muhammad sat on the right-hand side of the first seat in the front row. He was attired in his FOI suit and jeweled fez that he wore like no other. Men and women sat together. It was estimated approximately 200 cars caravanned in the procession to Mount Greenwood Cemetery, Thornton, Illinois, where Mother Marie was also interned. At the burial site, after services that consisted of prayers and condolences, the body of Mother Clara Muhammad was lowered in the ground while her husband, Elijah Muhammad, cried like a baby.

Granddaughter Halimah Muhammad-Ali reported, *"The day after my grandmother passed, my grandfather met with Muslims at 73rd and Stony Island and among other things said, 'My mission is over. Allah has shut my mouth. The one to come after me will bring a new religion altogether.'"* Another granddaughter, Amirah Muhammad, said, "My grandfather missed my grandmother to such a degree that after she passed away, he said, *'I will not live three (3) years beyond her death because I cannot go that long without her.'"* On February 25, 1975, the Honorable Elijah Muhammad passed, two years and six months after the passing of Clara Evans Muhammad.

PART 6: FROM MOTHER OF THE NATION TO MOTHER OF THE UMMAH

CHAPTER 15: THE SEED OF FATHER ABRAHAM AND THE FAITH OF MOTHER HAJAR

Clara Muhammad did not make Hajj or Umrah, but she believed in Allah, lived an honorable life, prayed, and read The Qur'an. Three remarkable communiques confirm her beliefs: *"An Invitation to 22 Million Black Americans"* published in the January 13, 1967, edition of *Muhammad Speaks* newspaper written by her; a letter to an MGT of Philadelphia, Pennsylvania written in her own hand December 1967; and the only known recording of a public address by Clara to a Washington, D.C. Muslim audience in her own voice. Clara undoubtedly believed her husband, Elijah Muhammad, was the Messenger of Allah to the Black man and woman in America. Still, she believed that Allah was G-D, The Supreme Being indicated in the above-cited references. Clara did not believe or mention in either communique G-D coming in the person of W. D. Fard Muhammad – that was the declaration of her husband.

Elijah deified his teacher in the 1930s for two reasons: 1) He initially believed W. D. Fard Muhammad was the prophesied Messiah spoken of in the Bible, and 2) he later used that position to advantage his efforts and ward off adversaries in the early establishment of the Allah Temple of Islam / *Lost Found Nation of Islam*. He expressed how he came to deify W. D. Fard Muhammad in his own words to Hatim Abdul Sahib in 1951,[204] in his first and most concise interview of the early days of the *Lost Found Nation of Islam.* Elijah reported that Fard's response to his elevation of him was: *That he was El Mahdi, the brother of Jesus, not Jesus.* But he also said to the masses, *Prophet was too big of a name for him.*

Clara revered W. D. Fard Muhammad and regarded him as the Saviour – inspired by G-D, Allah but not G-D, Allah. She opened her 1967 article stating, *"...I could write a book but I cannot put in words what Allah through his Messenger has done for me, Praise His Holy Name forever."* She closed her article saying, *"I have been following him (Messenger Elijah Muhammad) ever since he accepted Islam and I will follow him as long as I live, if it pleases Almighty G-D Allah, Praise His Holy Name forever."* Her praise after mentioning the name Allah is the same praise Muslims in the Ummah (universal community) offer after mentioning the name of Allah, only they do so in the Arabic language; Allah, *subhanawataAllah* (May Allah be Glorified Forever) is comparable to Allah, Praise his Holy Name forever.

In 1964, three years before Clara wrote her 1967 *Muhammad Speaks* article, her son Wallace was on the verge of being excommunicated from the Nation of Islam for the third time. She did not want him to be put out. It was during their conversation that he refused the demand of his father to say W. D. Fard Muhammad was G-D and the request of his mother to *"Just tell his father what he wanted to hear."* The irony is, Elijah taught his son from an early age the story of Luqman in The Qur'an[205], where it says: *"...Oh my son! Join not in worship others with Allah: for false worship is indeed the highest wrongdoing."* *"... Show gratitude to your parents, but if they strive to make you join in worship with Me things of which you/they have no knowledge, obey them not."*[206]

W. D. Fard Muhammad was greatly loved and appreciated by Clara and the early Muslims – Burnsteen Mohammed, Sally Allah, Viola Karriem, Mary Al-Manza, and others. None of them believed he was G-D. They called him the Saviour, and Clara fulfilled her promise to him. She nurtured her son, *the heir apparent*, Wallace (Imam W. Deen Mohammed), prophesied to be the next leader. Through this son, the Nation of Islam evolved, beginning in 1975. His dedicated study of the spiritual and psychological needs of Black people through the lens of The Qur'an enabled him to phase out language of the mythology of

W. D. Fard Muhammad and bring a new linguistic construction grounded in truth, revealed scripture and the Last Testament to humanity – The Qur'an.

Imam W. Deen Mohammed said, *"In real measure, the role of The Qur'an in my life is not without Clara Muhammad's attentive influence."*[207] Clara guided and protected her son, enabling him to study, make Umrah and Hajj, and connect to the great ancestral mother of all Muslims and humanity, Mother Hajar, peace be upon her. That connection enabled the narratives about Mother Hajar and Prophet(s) Abraham, Ishmael, and Noah, peace be upon them all, to be corrected. Rooted in both Revelation (Qur'an) and historical fact, the corrections eviscerated the Curse of Ham narrative and the debasement of Mother Hajar as a devalued slave woman depicted in the Biblical narrative of Hagar.

The correct history reflects high spiritual wisdom and reveals that the great ancestral mother was not commanded by G-D to be a slave to Sarah or any human being, or a sexual subordinate to Prophet Abraham/Ibrahim. Those demeaning narratives were written and put in the Bible Genesis by ancient Hebrew writers via their Midrash, who consistently rejected the Prophets and sought to elevate their ethnic group above all other people.

Mother Hajar was neither a slave nor a concubine; she was from noble, royal lineage, believed in One God, and her phenotype was dark skin. She came from the ancestors of Kemet and was given to Prophet Abraham/Ibrahim as a wife, not to Sarah as a slave. Allah chose her to be the womb to birth the first heir of Prophet Abraham/Ibrahim because of the purity of her faith and her character. She is memorialized forever in the ritual of Hajj. That was not the destiny of Sarah; the character of the two women revealed why Mother Hajar was chosen. When Mother Hajar conceived and birthed a male child, the jealousy of the Prophet's other wife, Sarah, made it impossible for her to live in peace. Mother Hajar's son was not a "wild ass of a man," as written in Genesis 16: 11-12. Ishmael was a Prophet and the first-born son of Prophet Abraham/Ibrahim.

It is important to remember that before religion was carved into numerous pieces and given various names, the purpose of Revelation and the work of the Prophets was to bring humanity from polytheism and idolatry to belief in One G-D. That remains the purpose of Revelation. Prophet Abraham/Ibrahim was ordered by the One G-D to take Mother Hajar to the desert in Arabia to establish a new community that would be obedient to G-D without jealously or conflict. When she was bewildered by her husband's actions, she said to him, recorded in the Hadith narrations:

> "O, Abraham! Where are you going, leaving us in this valley where there
> is no person whose company we may enjoy, nor is there anything (to enjoy)?"
> She repeated that to him many times, but he did not look back at her.
> She then asked him, "Has Allah ordered you to do so?" He said, "Yes."
> She said, "Then Allah will not neglect us."
>
> Abraham proceeded onwards, and on reaching the Thaniya (an elevated landmass similar to a hill) where they could not see him, he faced the Ka'ba (the original house built by Adam to the worship of One God, later rebuilt by Prophet Abraham and his son Ismail) and raising both hands invoked Allah saying the following prayer:
> Sahih Al-Bukhari Volume 4:583-584

The Qur'an confirms the Hadith with the following Revelation:
> "O our Lord! I have made some of my offspring dwell in a valley without
> cultivation, by Your Sacred House (Ka'ba at Makkah) in order, O our Lord,
> that they may establish perfect prayer. So fill the hearts of some among

them with love towards them, and (O Allah) provide them with fruits, so
that they may give thanks."
Qur'an - Surah Ibrahim (Abraham) - 14:37

Mother Hajar's faith enabled her to patiently persevere in the wilderness until G-D sent sustenance to her and her child in the form of water – *the Well of Zam Zam*. It continuously flows in Makkah as an underwater well, and its composition is like no other water on earth. As the founder of the *Well of Zam Zam*, Mother Hajar was able to draw people to build a community around her, which is now the city of Makkah, which she is also credited as founding. People of the Tribe of Jahume from the southern area now called Yemen were the first to settle in Makkah; they were Black people. Others came and were named Hajarites. Her faith and obedience to the One G-D and her allegiance to Prophet Abraham/ Ibrahim was before Prophet Muhammad, PPBUH was born, and before the Last Revelation, The Qur'an was revealed to him. Her ancient heritage from the area Kemet, now called Africa / Egypt, was the cradle of civilization where the belief in One G-D began with Prophet Adam. That belief was corrupted over time and began to be resumed with Pharaoh Akhenaten[208], also known as Amenhotep IV.

Mother Hajar raised her son, Prophet Ishmael/Ismail, to believe and reverence the One G-D. He and his father, Prophet Abraham/Ibrahim (re), built the Ka'ba –the first house built by Prophet Adam and re-dedicated to the worship of One G-D. The Biblical depiction of Prophet Ishmael in Genesis 16: 11-12 further confirms the malicious scheme to demean the Islamic lineage.

The presence of a woman with Black skin who believed in One G-D existed before Moses, Jesus, and Prophet Muhammad were born (prayers and peace be upon them all). Her dedication and obedience to G-D and her patient perseverance and striving are reenacted in the ritual of Hajj called *Saae'*. Mother Hajar is the only female so honored and the only person buried in the vicinity of the Ka'ba in Makkah.

Similar to Black history being hidden from the general population in America, the role of Black men and women in religious and Islamic history was also hidden from the world, complicated by lack of knowledge of other languages, particularly Aramaic, Hebrew, and Arabic. A Black woman named Barak, of Abyssinian parentage, was the wet nurse who suckled and cared for the baby Prophet Muhammad, PPBUH. When Al-Islam was formally established by name, the first convert was a woman, Khadijah bint Khuwaylid,[209] wife of Muhammad the Prophet. The first martyr in Al-Islam was a Black woman, Sumayyah bint Khubbat.[210] And the first trusted treasurer of Prophet Muhammad and muezzin (caller to prayer) of the new Muslim community was Bilal ibn Raba, a Black Ethiopian, barely mentioned in the voluminous Islamic literature until Clara's son, Imam W. Deen Mohammed, brought him forward. Although these names in Arabic suggest ethnic distance, these were people with lineages from Abyssinian/ Ethiopia, Kush/Kemet – they were of dark skin.

These corrections of history freed a people from mental, spiritual, and scriptural oppression, removing the mental anguish of inferiority. It enabled a people to realize they did not need myths to exalt themselves. G-D already distinguished Black people based on their obedience and faith. W. D. Fard Muhammad knew that his teaching was only to get the Black man and woman on their feet. And Clara's husband, Elijah, often said, *"My job is to clean you up. The one to come after me will teach you the religion."* Each knew that once the self-esteem of a people was awakened and the schemes that oppressed their development identified, The Qur'an would provide the guidance. They would learn that there is One G-D, who commissioned every Prophet and G-D's Covenant is with all humanity, not one single people. They would learn that G-D had already exalted them in their original creation [human identity] and in Islamic history even before the name Al-Islam was officially revealed in The Qur'an. But when it was revealed through Prophet Muhammad (PPBUH), it consolidated and corrected all scriptural guidance that came before it.

The Qur'an says in Surah/Chapter 5, ayat/verse 3:

*"This day have I perfected your religion for you
Completed My favor upon you,
And have chosen for you Al-Islam as your religion."*

The semi-circle to the right of the Ka'ba is called *The Skirt of Mother Hajar or The Lap of Mother Hajar*. Sound Tradition says this is where she nursed the baby Prophet Ishmael. In the performance of the rites of Hajj – Tawaf (circumambulation around the Ka'ba) – one shows respect for the Mother of the Ummah by not entering that space but going around it.

CHAPTER 16: THE MISSION OF WALLACE (IMAM W. DEEN MOHAMMED)

The Mujeddid

The mission of Clara's husband, Elijah Muhammad, was to break the psychological domination of white supremacy over Black people, to enable them to love themselves, think for themselves, and develop the discipline to create a world representing their own aspirations. His forty-four-year mission achieved unprecedented measurable results. Before Clara passed in 1972, she told Wallace, *"Son, go on and lead the people, they will follow you."*

The mission of Clara's son was to teach the correct concept of G-D (*aqidah*) and Human Identity in accord with the Universal Truths embodied in the Last Revelation – The Qur'an – thereby providing "psychic integrity" to followers suffering from cognitive dissonance resulting from conflicting identities as Black, American, minority, and Muslim.

Mujeddid is a concept in Al-Islam where once every century, a person is inspired by G-D to revive the faith to ensure the original principles outlined in The Qur'an and modeled by Prophet Muhammad (PPBUH) are being practiced. Al-Islam declares there is One G-D, One Humanity, One Creation, and One Brotherhood of Prophets sent to guide humanity. Upon assuming leadership after the passing of his father in 1975, Islamic scholar, Dr. Sulayman Nyang, Emeritus Professor Howard University, said of Clara's son: *"Like his father, Warithdeen deeply believed in the capacity and capability of the African-American and that their moral and social transformation was imperative. Two of his notable achievements were the Re-*

Islamization and the Re-Americanization of the movement."

Consistent with that goal, Imam Mohammed's 33-plus-year Mission accomplished introducing to the American conscious that The Qur'an declares G-D is not a man, black or white, and that Muslim life is based on the revealed word of G-D. Armed with the knowledge of Revelation – The Qur'a – he illuminated the man-made hierarchical structures that oppress all human society, of which color-consciousness/white supremacy is only one layer. The other more insidious layer is the false notion that G-D is a man from one ethnic group chosen above all others by G-D, thereby permitting them to enforce their will upon others without correction or consequence. The travesty of this misunderstanding of G-D and the Covenant was put in the Bible. The Qur'an was revealed to correct it.

To address this issue, in 1978, Imam Mohammed formed the Committee to Remove All Racial Images That Attempt to Portray the Divine (CRAID). Falsely interpreted by some as anti-Christian, Muslims and African Americans throughout America initiated a series of national lectures, articles, and conferences, illustrating from a clinical perspective the deleterious psychological effect of portraying the Divine in Caucasian flesh. (Since 1978, *Muslim Journal* newspaper continues to run a notice on page 2 titled, "A Message of Concern" explaining the detriment of this practice.)

Muslims demonstrated in silence in front of churches with signs explaining this correction. This dialogue resulted in the removal of the Caucasian image of G-D from numerous church premises and publications so that today, in most churches in America, particularly Black churches, the Caucasian image of G-D is gone, removed, due to this effort by the son of Clara Muhammad. The Association of Black Psychologists in 1980 headed by Dr. Na'im Akbar successfully approved and adopted the following resolution:[211] (partially presented): "*The portrayal of the Divine in images of Caucasian flesh constitutes an oppressive instrument destructive to the self-esteem of Black people throughout the world, supports the grandiosity of white supremacy, and is directly destructive to the psychological well-being of Black children."[212]*

> THEREFORE, BE IT RESOLVED: That the Association of Black Psychologists recommends the removal of all Caucasoid images of Divinity from public display and from places of worship, particularly in settings where young Black minds are likely to be exposed.[213] This was a groundbreaking accomplishment. – The World Community of Al-Islam in the West – WCIW

Without the perception of reality contained in The Qur'an, one is inclined to believe that a nation is larger and more significant than a community. On the contrary, a nation promotes nationalism, a singular commitment to a spatial/physical/ideological entity that can be right, wrong, or oppressive. The universal assemblage of Muslims is called Ummah (community), a more excellent, self-correcting body encompassing ethnicities of all people evolving on the principle of righteousness – obedience to G-D. In its unprecedented ideological shift from Nation to Community in 1976, Imam Mohammed renamed the Community, The World Community of Al-Islam in the West, stating, *"The Muslims in America should be promoting Community concerns. We are primarily, essentially, first and last a community, and are obligated to realize community life more than we are obligated to realize anything else."*

He then changed the flag of the Nation of Islam from the star and crescent to The Qur'an. The star and crescent are not mentioned in The Qur'an or the life of the Holy Prophet. It was raised in response to the Christian Cross during the Crusades. Muslims saw the cross as a sign of death and displayed the star and crescent as a sign of the heavens. This vision of The Qur'an as a flag was conceived by Elijah Muhammad. He said he saw a new book embedded with dimensional letters that glowed. The only letter he recognized was the Arabic letter 'lam.'

Imam Mohammed, in listening to his father's vision, questioned, *"What can this 'lam' stand for? I knew there was no other book coming to the Muslims after The Qur'an. Then it came to me. I said, My father is telling us that the new book to come is really a new book to us because we have never known the Holy Qur'an."* Imam Mohammed then created the flag and presented it to the Community, inspiring Sister Valita Sharif Muhammad of Chicago to create the first Muslim calendar incorporating the Islamic lunar year and the new Qur'an logo.

Published March 12, 1976, in the *Bilalian News*, it was the first time in Islamic history that The Qur'an was raised to symbolize Muslims, a Muslim country, and Muslim people, further demonstrating that Muslim African Americans were leaders in the Muslim world, not simply followers. Additionally, he stated that it is the prophetic destiny of African Americans to call all of humanity back to the worship of One G-D.

For 45 years (1930-1975), the Nation of Islam was the prime proponent of "Black" as an organizing principle, precipitated by the history of racial oppression. Acknowledging common African heritage, Imam Mohammed introduced the Community to the Muslim African Ancestor, Bilal ibn Rabah. Bilal was a slave to the Arabs who was liberated by Al-Islam. He became the First Treasurer and Muezzin (caller to prayer) of the first Muslim community. He was a trusted companion to Prophet Muhammad and would enter his living quarters and wake him for Morning Prayer.

Stating that *"Black"* lacked the depth and dignity required of a new people, Imam Mohammed coined the term *Bilalian* in his honor. Use of the term exposed that some believed that by embracing universal Al-Islam, the Community would be subsumed by another ethnic and religious governing authority. The fears were unfounded. Imam Mohammed said there are two things he would never give up: Al-Islam and his African-American identity. Some Muslims and other critics suggested he was developing a "cult" like his father. Therefore, the name *Bilalian* was used only for a short time.

Championing the Cause of Women - Reconstructing the Muslim Family and Community

One of the greatest attractions of the Nation of Islam was the sense of unity. Both Clara and Elijah championed the cause of women. Now with the right perception of G-D, knowledge of the value of both family and Community, life took on greater dimensions. With The Qur'an, Clara's son told women they were equal to men but also the *womb of mind* – that ultimately she was society because all life originates from her.

He evolved the male and female classes without conflict. FOI were encouraged to join Imam's Classes as head of households. They were required to learn The Qur'an – to guide their families in maintaining spiritual, physical, and financial discipline. MGT&GCC Classes were renamed, becoming Muslim Women's Development Class (MWDC), which encouraged women to pursue their G-D-given talents both in the home and into the broader society. CERWIS (The Committee to Enhance the Role of Women in Society) was established to address those social issues emerging in the 1970s and beyond that hindered the elevation of women. Citing Qur'anic support of male/female equality, he supported the Equal Rights Amendment and, in the 1970s, brought women into leadership positions, naming Amatullah Umrani as the first Instructress to teach both males and females.

Rawiyyah Khatib of New York City commented: *"I felt very liberated because of the knowledge he brought and because he respected the women. He opened the door to the intellectual side; it was not just a rote situation. Now, I admired the Honorable Elijah Muhammad too, he was the foundation. I remember the last Saviour's Day when he had white people and the man from Turkey on the stage...he said to respect everybody. He gave us dignity and respect as women and mothers. But Imam Mohammed allowed women to hold positions and their voices to be heard among the men and women, not just the women. It gave me courage to go to the warehouse (fish distribution center). And I got a job giving orders to men."*

The son of Clara Muhammad consistently gave lectures about his mother, citing her faithful dedication and commitment to Education. *"My mother would save up over the year, and when it was time for students to graduate, she would always have some money to give them special gifts. More important than the flowers or gifts was that look on her face of satisfaction and encouragement that said: 'Son, you made me so happy. I am behind you to keep doing what you are doing.' The smile would light up her face and make you feel so good and rewarded for what you have done that she appreciated. And I saw her give that same look to the children that were not of her own blood. She would give them that same look that was not in any way different than the look she would give to me. I want the children of Sister Clara Muhammad schools to know that."*

The Clara Muhammad Memorial and Educational Foundation, founded by Clara's daughter-in-law Shirley Muhammad, in December 1976, provided immeasurable support for education by keeping the legacy of Clara Muhammad alive. The ritual of giving flowers and gifts to graduates was continued, as was providing scholarships for Clara Muhammad School students and those entering college. The expansion of cultural activities and gala banquets enriched the Muslim community. The Foundation also reproduced audiotapes of the lectures of Imam W. Deen Mohammed. Unfortunately, after many years of request, Mrs. Shirley Mohammed declined to be interviewed for this book.

A Healthy Patriotism

In his book *Journey into America: The Challenge of Islam 2010*, Dr. Akbar Ahmed (former Ambassador to Pakistan and Chair of Islamic Studies – American University, Washington, D.C.) said: *"The genius of Imam W.D. Mohammed was that he single-handedly moved the African-American toward identifying with pluralist American identity while moving away from Black Nationalist Islam. Today, millions of African-American Muslims are comfortable with being as strongly American as they are being devout Muslims, demonstrating that the two are not incompatible. This achievement is due entirely to Imam W.D. Mohammed."*[214]

In July 1977, Imam Mohammed lifted up the American flag, told his supporters to vote, and established New World Patriotism Day as an annual celebration. For the first time in American history (23 August 1984), over 10,000 Muslims gathered around the Washington Monument on the National Mall for the first-ever "Muslim Political Convention." Imam Mohammed spoke of "The Earth-Our Home", promoting responsibility for the earth and its environment, and also on "Building Political Responsibility", in which he stated that allegiance to a country has little to do with the conduct of the government or attitude of citizens, but more with their determination to stand for justice, thereby enabling them to evolve into their full humanity, which Al-Islam invites them to.

After being the first Muslim to offer the invocation to the United States Senate (February 6, 1992), Imam Mohammed was later honored with a 500-guest reception at the Pentagon. Invited to both Presidential Inaugural Prayer Services by President William Jefferson Clinton, Imam Mohammed was observed by Taylor Branch, the Pulitzer Prize winning biographer of Martin Luther King, Jr., who was also present at the 1993 Service at the Metropolitan AME Church in Washington. D.C. Branch wrote in his book: *"Among the speakers came Imam Wallace D. Mohammed, reciting Qur'anic verses of peace in Arabic and English...In a book review he had expressed to me his long-term ambition for Muslim Americans to help reconcile world Islam with democracy. I considered Mohammed the Nation's most underappreciated religious figure of the 20th Century."*[215]

Reaffirmed Al-Islam As Part of the American Religious Tradition

Attended by Presidents Jimmy Carter, Gerald Ford, the Reverend Billy Graham, and Mrs. Coretta Scott King, among others, the Williamsburg Charter Foundation's "First Liberty" Reaffirmation Ceremony for the Freedom of Religion (June 25, 1988) had one Muslim signatory – Imam W. Deen Mohammed. The signature of Clara's son ensured that America is not only a Judeo-Christian but a Judeo/Christian/Muslim country consistent with the faith tradition of Monotheism.

Clara's son had an interfaith relationship with the Focolare Movement of the Catholic Church and Lady Chiara Lubrich that was unprecedented. She recalled, *"We have had many meetings with our Muslim friends. What characterizes these gatherings above all is the presence of God, which one notices when they pray and which gives much hope. I saw this hope become a reality in the Malcolm Shabazz Mosque in Harlem (USA) years ago when I was invited to explain my Christian experience to 3,000 African-American Muslims. Their welcome, beginning with that of their leader, Imam W. D. Mohammed, was so warm, sincere, and enthusiastic that it led us to great expectations for the future."*[216]

In 1975 America, materialism, immorality, and heightened sexuality swept the country in a culture the Pope of Rome later called "A Culture of Death." The revivalist message for all faiths to return to their sacred origins, initiated by the son of Clara Muhammad, was welcomed by numerous religious leaders. His interfaith relations among Jews, Christians, Muslims, and other faith traditions greatly influenced an American culture, questioning not only the existence but the need for G-D as reflected in the *Time* magazine, April 1966, cover, *"Is God Dead?"*

Joshua Haberman, Senior Rabbi Emeritus of the Washington Hebrew Congregation, in 1992, said, *"Imam W. Deen Mohammed is one of the most enlightened religious leaders in our world today. He is a pioneer in developing good relations between Muslims and Jews in America dramatized by our historic pulpit exchange in Washington and Chicago in 1978. I am deeply impressed by his spiritual leadership and pray for G-D's blessings upon his good work."*[217]

At the invitation from Pope John Paul II in 1999, Imam W. Deen Mohammed became both the first Muslim and African-American to speak from the Vatican pulpit to a televised global audience of millions. After mentioning the honorable intentions of his father and citing the concept of One Humanity, he taught from Qur'an 49:13 (5), *"O humanity, We created you from a single male and female, and made you into nations and tribes, that you may know each other. Indeed the most honored of you in the sight of G-D is the most conscious of you, and G-D has full knowledge and is well acquainted with all things."*

Clara began her life as a Christian, and her son, sensitive to the relationship between Muslim African Americans and the larger African-American community, stated: *"We are not to separate from African-American Christians and those Christian leaders who got us as far as we have gotten before we reconnected to The Qur'an and the life of the Prophet. We are brothers and sisters in humanity as a people descended from African parents who were enslaved and oppressed in these United States..."* In the early 1980s, he declared: *"Two things I will never give up, my Al-Islam and my African-American-ness."*

Muslim African-American Independence

The emphasis Imam Mohammad placed on the Revival of Religion included a devastating critique of a global Muslim world mired in polemical issues and not demonstrating the historical excellence of Muslim tradition, as exemplified in the life of the Holy Prophet. Refusing to align this new community of Muslims in America with any foreign government, religious tradition, or ideology, he stated: *"We only support the good they do."*

In rejecting Orientalist terminology such as "orthodox Islam" and sectarian labels such as Sunni/Shia/Sufi/Salafi, etc., he stated that only the *"Uswaah"* (character) of Prophet Mohammed was worthy of emulation. As a special guest of Iranian President Rafsanjani at the Organization of Islamic Conference (OIC), in Tehran, Iran, in 1997 – in working to erase distinctions between those called "Sunni" and "Shia" – he reminded the assembled gathering of Muslim heads of state that these distinctions did not exist during the life of the Prophet.

At a 2000 conference at the Interdenominational Theological Seminary in Atlanta, Georgia, Clara's son was asked whether or not he believed Muslim African Americans should have their own 'madhab' (School of Islamic thought). He responded: *"Yes, I believe it more now than when I said it several years ago. Why? Because when we study the development of these madhabs for Muslims in the old world (i.e., Africa, Saudi Arabia, and other places), we find they had more in common than we have with them now – being 1,000+years and a continent away in a very new human American society. They need to re-study their "madhabs" in light of the changes that have come about on Earth. For us in America, G-D has restored life to the empty vessel of those enslaved children, thereby creating a new people in society on this Planet Earth. We are a new people born out of Revelation – The Qur'an. We did not exist before. So, we are new thinkers. We don't think like Arabs, we don't think like Asians, we think like 'us.' We don't think like white people, we don't think like Africans, we think like us. Now, why should the Islamic world be deprived of Al-Islam being expressed through this new and innocent vessel?"*

Three years after the death of Clara Muhammad (1975), the world witnessed the largest conversion to Al-Islam in the 20th century. Within two years (1977), her son led the largest delegation ever of Muslim Americans to Hajj (Pilgrimage to Mecca). Clara's son was honored by being designated the *Khatib* (lecturer and leader of prayer) on Mount Arafat, where Prophet Mohammed delivered his last address. Imam W. Deen Mohammed often said, *"My mother passed in 1972 and I still listen to her."* His nephew, Hasan Sharif, added, *"To comfort me after the death of my mother, Ethel, in 2002, he spoke of his connection to*

Grandmother Clara. He told me he talks to her all the time. He said to me, 'I say, Mama, I'm still on the job, working hard.'"

IMAGES

Clara Evans Muhammad and son, Wallace (Imam W. Deen Mohammed), at four years old. Photo Courtesy: Nathaniel Muhammad

The Children of Clara and Elijah Muhammad - Left to right standing: Ethel, Emmanuel, Lottie Rayya, Nathaniel, Seated left to right: Herbert Jabir, Wallace, Elijah, Jr. (Not included Akbar Muhammad). Photo Courtesy: Nathaniel Muhammad

Marie Poole Muhammad, Mother-in-Law of Clara Muhammad. Photos courtesy: Nathaniel Muhammad

Elijah and Clara Muhammad, Wedding Anniversary, Courtesy: Nathaniel Muhammad

Clara Muhammad Serving Food for a Family Gathering at her home, Sister Francis Assisting. Halimah Muhammad far right. Courtesy: Amatullah Okapu Sharieff

Clara Muhammad (Center) with Granddaughters Right to Left: Salma, Clara Muhammad, Regina, and Ruqaiyah. Photo Courtesy: Ozier Muhammad

KEY FIGURES

Clara Muhammad's Children

Emmanuel Muhammad (1921-1998)
Ethel Muhammad Sharrieff (1922-2002)
Lottie Muhammad (1925-2017)
Nathaniel Muhammad (1926-2017)
Herbert [Jabir] Muhammad (1929-2008)
Elijah Muhammad, Jr. (1931-2020)
Wallace Delaney Muhammad [Imam Warith Deen Mohammad] (1933-2008)
Dr. Akbar Muhammad (1939-2016)

Other Individuals

Kallat Muhammad, the brother of Elijah Muhammad who opposed his leadership.

BIBLIOGRAPHY

Lectures

Johnson, Mordecai Wyatt. "The Faith of the American Negro." Commencement Address to Harvard University, July 19, 1922.

Muhammed, W. Deen. Address to Interdenominational Theological Seminary, Atlanta, GA. April, 2000.

Music / Songs

Barton, William E. "Sometime I Feel Like a Motherless Child." 1899.

References

'Ali,'Abdullah Yusuf. The Meaning of The Holy Qur'an. Eleventh Edition. Amana Publications, Beltsville, MD, 2008

An-Nawawi's. *Forty Hadith – An Anthology of the Sayings of The Prophet Muhammad* (saws) Sautul Islam Publications, Inc. 1988. Princeton, NJ.

Christopher Manning, "African Americans", Encyclopedia of Chicago, http://www.encyclopedia/chicagohistory.org/pages/27

Encyclopedia Britannica. "Early Modern Plantation Slavery." Macropedia. vols. 9 and 16. Chicago, IL: 1973-74, 860-863.

Encyclopedia of Chicago 2004 The Newberry Library; See also The Electronic Encyclopedia of Chicago, 2005; Chicago Historical Society.

Encyclopedia of Seerah Volume 2. Seerah Foundation London, 1987.

Forty Hadith – An Anthology of the Sayings of The Prophet Muhammad (saws) by Al-Nawawi. Sautul Islam Publications, Inc. 1988. Princeton, NJ. Hadith #2.

Lane, Edward William. Arabic-English Lexicon. London: Williams & Norgate, 1863.

Ma'Ariful Quran. Volume 1. Maulana Mufti Muhammad Shafi. Karachi, 1996.

Muhammad, W. D. Fard. *Supreme Wisdom*, 1930.

Oxford English Dictionary: http://www.oed.com/view/Entry/152685?redirectedFrom=prophecy#eid

Random House Dictionary, Classic Edition, New York, 1983.

Sahih Bukhari, Arabic/English, DarussSalaam, Riyad, Saudi Arabia, 1997.

Slave Rebellions: U.S. and Slave Trade, 266- 267.

Supreme Wisdom by W. D. Fard Muhammad, 1930.

The Honorable Wives of the Prophet (Prayers and Peace Be Upon Him). Editor, Abdul Ahad. Maktaba Darus-Salam, Research & Compilation Department, Riyadh, Jeddah, London, New York, 2004.

The Modern King James Version of the Holy Bible. Translated by Jay P. Green, 1962.

The New International Version Rainbow Study Bible. El Reno, Oklahoma: Rainbow Studies, Inc., 1996.

The Translation of the Meanings of Sahih Al-Bukhari, Arabic-English, Volume 1. Darussalam, Riyadh, Saudi Arabia, 1997.

US Department of State Office of the Historian http://history.state.gov/

Zarabozo, Jamaal al-Din M. Commentary on the Forty Hadith

of Al-Nawawi. Volume 1. Al-Basheer Center for Publication and Translations, Denver, CO, 1998.

Books

Akbar, Na'im. *Chains and Images of Psychological Slavery*. Jersey City: New Mind Productions, 1984.

Ahmed, Akbar. *Journey Into America: The Challenge of Islam*. Brookings Institution Press, Washington, D.C., 2010.

Anderson, James D. *The Education of Blacks in the South 1860-1935*. Chapel Hill: University of North Carolina, 1988.

Austin, Allan D. *African Muslims in Antebellum America – Transatlantic Stories and Spiritual Struggles*. New York: Routledge, 1997.

Baldwin, James. *The Fire Next Time*. New York: Dell Publishing Company, 1962.

Baptist, Edward. The Half Has Not Been Told: Slavery and the Making of American Capitalism. Philadelphia: Perseus Books Group, 2014.

Barboza, Steven. American Jihad: Islam After Malcolm X. Image Books, Doubleday. New York, 1994.

Bilal, Rafiq and Thomas Goodwin. *Egyptian Sacred Science in Islam*. Bennu Publishers, San Francisco, 1985.

Billingsley, Andrew. *Climbing Jacob's Ladder: The Enduring Legacies of African American Families*. New York: Touchstone Simon & Schuster, 1992.

Blassingame, John W. *The Slave Community: Plantation Life in the Antebellum South*. New York: Oxford University Press, 1972, 1979.

Blyden, Edward Wilmot. *Christianity, Islam and the Negro Race,*

1887. Martino Publishing, Mansfield Centre, CT, 2006.

Branch, Taylor. *Pillar of Fire: America In The King Years 1963-65*. Simon & Shuster, New York, 1998.

Brizendine, Louann. *The Female Brain*. New York: Morgan Road Books, 2006.

Brodkin, Karen. How Jews Became White Folks. New Jersey: Rutgers University Press, 1998.

Broughton, Virginia W. "The Social Status of the Colored Women and its Betterment" in *The United Negro: His Problems and His Progress* I. Edited by Garland Penn and J.W. E. Bowen, 450. Atlanta: D.E. Luther Publishing, 1902.

Brown, Nikki and Barry Stentiford. *The Jim Crow Encyclopedia: Greenwood Milestones in African American History*. Westport: Greenwood Press, 2008.

Cantril, Hadley. *The Psychology of Social Movements*. John Wiley & Sons, Inc.: New York, 1941.

Clegg 3rd, Claude Andrew. *An Original Man - The Life and Times of Elijah Mohammed*. New York: St. Martin's Press, 1997.

Cooper, Anna Julia. *A Voice From the South By a Black Woman of the South*. Xenia, Ohio: The Aldine Printing House, 1892.

Diouf, Sylviane A. *Servants of Allah – African Muslims Enslaved in the Americas*. New York: New York University Press, 1998.

Dittmer, John. *Black Georgia in the Progressive Era 1900-1920*. Chicago: University of Illinois Press, 1977.

Douglass, Frederick. *My Bondage and My Freedom*. New York: Miller, Orton & Mulligan, 1855. New York: Dover Publications, 1969.

DuBois, W. E. B., Ed. *The Negro Church: Report of a Social Study Made Under the Direction of Atlanta University: Together with the*

Proceedings of the Eighth Conference for the Study of the Negro Problems... held at Atlanta University, May 26th, 1903. Rowman AltaMira, 1903.

Du Bois, W. E. B. and Augustus Granville Dill, eds. *The College-Bred Negro American.* Atlanta: Atlanta University, 1902.

DuBois, W. E. B. *The Souls of Black Folk.* Chicago: A.C. McClurg and Company, 1903.

DuBois, W. E. B. *Black Reconstruction in America 1860-1880.* New York: The Free Press, 1962.

DuBois, W. E. B. The World and Africa: International Publishers, New York, 1946.

Du Bois. W. E. B. *The Autobiography of W.E.B. DuBois.* New York: International Publishers, 1968.

Essien-Udom, E.U. *Black Nationalism: A Search for an Identity in America.* Chicago: University of Chicago Press, 1962.

Evanzz, Karl. *The Messenger – The Rise and Fall of Elijah Mohammed.* New York: Pantheon Books, 1999.

Fanon, Franz. *Black Skin, White Masks.* 1952. New York: Grove Press, 2008.

Fanon, Franz. *The Wretched of the Earth.* 1963. New York: Grove Press, 2004.

Fauset, Arthur Huff. *Black Gods of the Metropolis.* Philadelphia Anthropological Society: University of Pennsylvania Press, 1944.

Feuerlicht, Strauss Roberta. *The Fate of the Jews: A People Torn Between Israeli Power and Jewish Ethics.* New York: Times Books, 1983.

Ford, Henry and Samuel Crowther. *My Life and Work.* Garden City, NY: Garden City Publishing Company, 1922.

Freire, Paulo. *Pedagogy of the Oppressed.* New York: Continuum Publishing, 1986.

Franklin, John Hope. *The Emancipation Proclamation.* New York: Doubleday and Company, 1963.

Franklin, John Hope. *From Slavery to Freedom: The History of Negro Americans.* New York: McGraw-Hill, Inc., 1947. Alfred A. Knopf, 2000.

Franklin, John Hope and Harriet Pipes McAdoo. *Introduction to Black Families.* Thousand Oaks, CA: Sage Publications Inc., 2007.

Frazier, E. Franklin. *The Negro Family in the United States,* 1939. Chicago: Univ. of Chicago; Revised and Abridged Ed. New York: The Dryden Press, 1948.

Frazier, E. Franklin. *Black Bourgeoisie.* The Free Press, 1957, 1985; Macmillan Company, Simon & Schuster, Inc. New York, 1990.

Giddings, Paula. *When and Where I Enter: The Impact of Black Women on Race and Sex in America.* New York: William Morrow and Co., 1984.

Goetz, Rebecca Anne. *The Baptism of Early Virginia: How Christianity Created Race.* Baltimore: John Hopkins University Press, 2012.

Goldenberg, David M. *The Curse of Ham: Race and Slavery in Early Judaism, Christianity and Islam.* Princeton, New Jersey: Princeton University Press, 2003.

Gordon-Reed, Annette. *Thomas Jefferson and Sally Hemings: An American Controversy.* Charlottesville: University of Virginia Press, 1997.

Gutman, Herbert G. *The Black Family in Slavery and Freedom 1750-1925.* New York: Pantheon Books, 1976.

Harlan, Louis R. "Booker T. Washington's Discovery of Jews"

in *Region, Race and Reconstruction*, Edited by J. Morgan Kousser and James M. McPherson, 268-284. New York: Oxford University Press, 1982.

Helper, Hinton Rowan. *Negroes in Negroland, Negroes in America and Negroes Generally*. New York: G.W. Carlton, 1868.

Herrnstein, Richard and Charles Murray. *The Bell Curve - Intelligence and Class Structure in American Life*. New York: Free Press, 1994.

Hill, Robert. *Research on The African-American Family - A Holistic Perspective*. Boston: William Monroe Trotter Institute, 1993.

Hine, Darlene Clark and Kathleen Thompson. *A Shining Thread of Hope - The History of Black Women in America*. New York: Broadway Books, 1998.

Jackson, Keneth T. *Ku Klux Klan in the City 1915-1930*. Chicago: Oxford University Press, 1964.

Jefferson, Thomas. *Notes on the State of Virginia*. Boston: Lilly and Wait, 1832.

Johnson, Christine. *Muhammad's Children: A First Grade Reader*. University of Islam, Chicago, 1963.

Johnson, Whittington B. *Black Savannah, 1788-1864*. University of Arkansas Press, 1996.

Kipling, Rudyard. *The White Man's Burden*, 1899.

Koshak, Yahya Hamza. *Zamzam: The Holy Water*. Koshak Research Institute, Inc. Jeddah, Saudi Arabia, 1983 in Arabic, in English, 1999.

Lemert, Charles and Esme Bhan. *The Voice of Anna Julia Cooper*. New York: Rowman and Littlefield, 1998.

Lincoln, C. Eric. *The Black Muslims in America*. Boston: Beacon Press, 1961.

Lomax, Louis E. *When the Word is Given*. New York: Signet Books - New American Library, 1963.

Marsh, Clifton E. *From Black Muslims to Muslims: The Transition from Separatism to Islam, 1930-1980*. Metuchen, N. J and London: The Scarecrow Press, Inc. 1984.

Martin, Elizabeth Anne. "Religion and the Immigrant." *In Detroit and the Great Migration 1916-1929*. Bentley Historical Library, University of Michigan, 1993.

Martin, Elizabeth Anne. "Institutions in Detroit: Answering the Call of Migrant Needs." *In Detroit and the Great Migration 1916-1929*. Bentley Historical Library, University of Michigan, 1993.

Melamed, Abraham. *The Image of the Black in Jewish Culture*. London, 2003.

McCloud, Aminah Beverly. *African American Islam*. New York: Routledge, 1995.

Montagu, Ashley. *The Natural Superiority of Women*. Rev. ed. New York: Macmillan, 1968.

Moore, Dan, Sr. and Michelle Mitchell. *Black Codes in Georgia*. The APEX Museum, Atlanta, 2006.

Morrison, Toni. *The Bluest Eye.* Vintage International, Random House, New York, 1970.

Muhammad, Akbar. "Muslims in the United States: An Overview of Organizations, Doctrines and Problems." In *The Islamic Impact*. Edited by Yvonne Haddad, Byron Haines and Ellison Findly. Syracuse: Syracuse University Press, 1984.

Muhammad, Akbar. "Some Factors Which Promote and Restrict Islamization in America." *The American Journal of Islamic Studies* 1 (1984).

Muhammad, Amir Nashid Ali. *Muslims in America – Seven Centuries of History (1312-2000)*. Beltsville, MD: Amana Publications, 1998.

Muhammad, Elijah. *Message to the Blackman in America*. Chicago: Temple No. 2 Publications, 1965.

Muhammad, Mary'yam T., Tauheed B. Muhammad and Burnsteen Mohammed. *A Step in The Right Direction- The Missing Link*. Pioneers Publishing Committee: Detroit, Michigan, 1993.

Muhammad, W. Deen. *An African American Genesis*. Calumet City, IL: M.A.C.A. Publication Fund, 1986.

Myrdal, Gunnar. *An American Dilemma: The Negro Problem and Modern Democracy*. New York: Harper and Brothers, 1944.

Patterson, James T. *Brown v. Board of Education: A Civil Rights Milestone and Its Troubled Legacy*. New York: Oxford University Press, 2001.

Patterson, James T. *Brown v. Board: Its Impact on Education, and What it Left Undone*. African–American Studies at the Woodrow Wilson Center.

Pettigrew, Thomas F. *Epitaph for Jim Crow*. New York: Anti-Defamation League of B'nai B'rith, 1964.

Ragg, Lonsdale and Laura Ragg. *The Gospel of Barnabas*. Cedar Rapids, Iowa: Unity Publishing Company, 1973.

Ransby, Barbara. *Ella Baker & the Black Freedom Movement*. Chapel Hill: The University of North Carolina Press, 2003.

Ross, Rosetta E. *Witnessing and Testifying – Black Women, Religion and Civil Rights*. Minneapolis: Fortress Press, 2003.

Sahib, Hatim A. *The Nation of Islam*. M.A. Thesis, University of Chicago, 1951.

Salzman, Jack and Cornel West. *Struggles in the Promised Land,*

New York 1997.

Schappes, Morris U. *A Documentary History of the Jews in the United States*. New York: Citadel Press, 1950.

Schleifer, Aliah. *Motherhood in Islam*. Cambridge, UK: The Islamic Academy, 1986.

Scott, Ellsworth. *Death in a Promised Land, The Tulsa Race Riot of 1921*. Baton Rouge: Louisiana State University Press, 1982.

Segal, Ronald. *Islam's Black Slaves: the Other Black Diaspora*. New York: Farrar, Straus, Giroux, 2001.

Shariati, Ali. *Hajj*. Evecina Cultural & Education Foundation, Jubilee Press, Costa Mesa, California, 3rd Edition, 1993.

Silverman, J.H. "The Law of the Land is the Law: Antebellum Jews, Slavery and the Old South" in Struggles in the Promised Land: Toward a History of Black-Jewish Relations in the United States. New York: Oxford University Press, 1997, p. 73-86.

Stampp, Kenneth M. The Peculiar Institution Slavery in the Antebellum South. New York: Vintage Books, Random House, 1956.

Sudarkasa, Niara. *The Strength of Our Mothers: African and African American Women and Families: Essays and Speeches*. Trenton, NJ: Africa World Press Inc., 1996.

Swartley, Willard M. *Slavery, Sabbath, War and Women: Case Issues in Biblical Interpretation*. Scottsdale, PA: Herald Press, 1983.

Talmay, Stewart E. and E. M. Beck. *A Festival of Violence: An Analysis of Southern Lynching 1882-1930*. Champaign, IL: University of Illinois Press, 1995.

Teubal, Savina J. *Hagar The Egyptian: The Lost Tradition of the Matriarchs*. Harper Collins, New York, 1990.

Thurman, Howard. *With Head and Heart: The Autobiography of Howard Thurman.* Harcourt Brace Jovanovich, New York, 1979

Turner, Richard Brent. *Islam in the African-American Experience.* Bloomington: Indiana University Press, 1997.

Tuttle, William. *Race Riot: Chicago in the Red Summer of 1919.* Chicago: Illini Books, 1996.

Van Evrie, J.H., M.D. *Negroes and Negro "Slavery," The First an Inferior Race: The Latter Its Normal Condition.* Baltimore: John D. Goy, 1863.

Van Sertima, Ivan. *They Came Before Columbus.* New York: Random House, 1976.

Van Sertima, Ivan, ed. "Golden Age of the Moor." *Journal of African Civilizations,* Vol. 2. 1991. New Brunswick, London: Transaction Publishers, 1992.

Wald, Elijah. Talking 'Bout Your Mama: The Dozens, Snaps and the Deep Roots of Rap. Oxford University Press, 2014.

Walker, David. *David Walker's Appeal to the Coloured Citizens of the World.* 1830. Baltimore, MD: Black Classic Press, 1993.

Wallace-Sanders, Kimberly. *Mammy – A Century of Race, Gender and Southern Memory.* Ann Arbor: University of Michigan Press, 2008.

Watkins, Williams. The White Architects of Black Education: Ideology and Power in America, 1865-1954: New York, Teachers College Press, 2001.

Webb, Clive. *A History of Black-Jewish Relations in the American South, 1790-1970.* Ph.D. Diss., University of Cambridge, 1997.

Wells-Barnett, Ida B. *Southern Horrors: Lynch Law in All Its Phases.* The New York Age Print, 1892.

Wells-Barnett, Ida B. *The Red Record – Tabulated Statistics and*

Alleged Causes of Lynching in the United States. 1895.

Wilkerson, Isabel. *The Warmth of Other Suns.* New York: Random House, 2010.

Wilson, Joseph. *The Elite of Our People: Sketches of Black Upper-Class Life in Antebellum Philadelphia,* 1841.

Winchell, Alexander, LLD. *Proof of Negro Inferiority.* Sons of Liberty, 1880, 1983.

Wolcott, Victoria W. *Remaking Respectability - African-American Women in Interwar Detroit.* Chapel Hill: The University of North Carolina Press, 2001.

Woodson, Carter G. *The Education of the Negro Prior to 1861 – A History of the Education of the Colored People of the United States from the Beginning of Slavery to the Civil War,*
1919.

Woodson, Carter G. *The Mis-Education of the Negro.* 1933. Drewryville, VA: H. Khalif Khalifah, 2006.

Wright, Richard Robert. *A Brief Historical Sketch of Negro Education in Georgia.* Robenson Printing House, 1894.

Articles

Aaron, David. "Early Rabbinic Exegesis on Noah's Son Ham and the So-Called 'Hamitic Myth." Journal of the American Academy of Religion 63 (1995).

Atlanta Constitution (April 25, 1901).

Atlanta Constitution (Oct. 10, 1913).

Atlanta Journal (Jan. 15, 1915).

Beynon, Erdmann Doane. "The Voodoo Cult Among Negro Migrants in Detroit." *American Journal of Sociology* 43, no. 6 (May,

1938): 894-907. University of Chicago Press.

Bishop, Cindy. "Former Holsey-Cobb Institute to Hold Reunion." *Cordele Dispatch* (July 24, 2007).

Booker T. Washington's Discovery of Jews" in *Region, Race and Reconstruction*. Eds. J. Morgan Kousser and James M. McPherson, (New York, Oxford University Press), 1982,

Brown, Eugene. "Nineteen Slain in Florida Race War." *The Chicago Defender* (January 13, 1923).

"The Black Scholar." *The Black Scholar Interviews Alex Haley* Volume 8, No. 1 (September, 1976): 33- 40.

Christopher Manning, "African Americans", Encyclopedia of Chicago, http://www.encyclopedia/chicagohistory.org/pages/27
"A Community Transformed: African-American Women and Detroit's Great Migration" For the Institute for Detroit Studies presentation, "A City of Women: Detroit in the 1920s."

Chimezie, Amuczie. "The Dozens: An African-Heritage Theory". Journal of Black Studies, Vol 6, No. 4, pp. 401-420, June, 1976.

The Crisis 5 (February 1913). New York: NAACP, 165; (March, 1913): 279.

The Crisis 9 (February 1915). New York: NAACP, 182; (March, 1915): 225-228.

Crisp County's History in Pictures and Stories. Contributor Cordele-Crisp County Historical Society. Atlanta: W. H. Wolfe Associates, Atlanta: 1978, 480.

Crowe, Charles. "Racial Massacre in Atlanta: September 22, 1906." *Journal of Negro History* 54 (April, 1969).

Dollard, John. "The Dozens: Dialectic of Insult" in Alan Dundes (editor) Mother Wit from the Laughing Barrell. University Press of Mississippi, 1973. P. 277-294.

DuBois, W. E. B. "The Atlanta Conferences." *Voice of the Negro* 1 (March, 1904).

DuBois, W. E. B. "Does the Negro Need Separate Schools?" 4 Journal of Negro Education, Vol No. 3, July, 1935. pp 328-329. p. 328-335, July, 1935.

Dye, Thomas R. "Rosewood, Florida: The Destruction of an African-American Community." *The Historian* 58, no.3 (Spring 1996).

Georgia Department of Natural Resources Historic Preservation Division African-American. georgiashpo.org/historic/African-American

Hellwig, David J. "Black Images of Jews: From Reconstruction to Depression." *Societas*, no. 3 (Summer, 1978).

Journal of Presbyterian History 53, no 3. (Fall, 1975): 219-222.

"Last Negro Homes Razed – Rosewood: Florida Mob Deliberately Fires One House After Another in Black Section." *The New York Times* (January 8, 1923).

Lefever, Harry. "Playing the Dozens: A Mechanism for Social Control". Phylon, Vol. 42, No. 1 pp. 73-85, Spring, 1981.

Lincoln, C. Eric. "The Muslim Mission in the Context of American Social History." African-American Religion: Interpretive Essays in History and Culture. T.E. Fulop & A.J. Raboteau, Routledge, New York, 1997, p. 288.

Mazrui, Ali A. "The Dual Memory, Genetic and Factual." *Transition Exchange*, no. 57 (Indiana University Press, 1992): 134-146.

McCloud, Aminah Beverly. "African-American Muslim Intellectual Thought." Souls: A Critical Journal of Black Politics, *Culture and Society* 9, no 2 (2007): 171-181.

McElroy, Susan Williams and Kruti Dholakia, "Between Plessy and Brown: Georgia School Finance in 1910," Southern Economic Association, 75th Annual Meeting, Washington, D.C. November 18, 2005. (University of Texas at Dallas): 5 and 7.

Mencken, H. L. *American Mercury* (February, 1926).

Murray, Benjamin and Mary O. Williams. "A History of Gillespie-Selden Institute From 1902-1915" in *Crisp County's History in Pictures and Stories.* Contributor Cordele-Crisp County Historical Society. Atlanta: W. H. Wolfe Associates, Atlanta: 1978

Peeks, Edward. "An Oasis in the Land of Jim Crow." *Journal Constitution* (March 12, 1989): 1D, 4D, 5D.

Pierce, David H. "Is the Jew a Friend of the Negro?" *The Crisis* 30 (August, 1925): 184.

Rashid, Hakim and Zakiyyah Muhammed. "The Sister Clara Muhammed Schools: Pioneers in the Development of Islamic Education in America." Journal of Negro Education, 61:2, 1992.

Savannah Tribune (January 23, 30, 1915).

The South Georgia News (July, 2006): 10.

"Spotlighting Historic Gillespie-Selden." *The South Georgia News* (July, 2006): 10.

"The Old Mammy Market." *The New York Times* (January 9, 1908): 8.

The Saks and Company advertisement (tunics in nigger brown). *The New York Times* (August 23, 1914): 11.

Webb, C. "Jewish Merchants and Black Customers in the Age of Jim Crow". Southern Jewish History, Vol. 2, pp. 55-80, 1999.

Interviews

AbuBakr, Harriett Mohammed. Interview with author. Telephone interview. Anaheim, CA. January 20, 2011. Personal interview. Atlanta, GA. September 27, 2012.

Al Kitab, Rawiyah. Interview with author. Telephone Interview. Anaheim, California. December 6, 2012.

Brogdon, Debra (Librarian, Cordele-Crisp Carnegie Library, Cordele, GA). Interview with author. Telephone interview. Anaheim, CA. January 12, 2011; Personal interview. Cordele, GA. September 27, 2011.

Farrakhan, Minister Louis. Interview with author. Telephone Interview. Anaheim, CA. August 5, 2010.

Karim, Darnell. Interview with author. Personal Interview. Chicago, IL. February 4, 1991; Telephone interview. Anaheim, CA. February 12, 2011; January 29, 2014.

Karim, Gloria. Interview with author. Telephone interview. Anaheim, CA. November 11, 2013.

Mahmoud, Tauheedah. Interview with author. Telephone interviews. Anaheim, CA. February 2, 6, 7, 12, 2007.

Maurad, Beverly. Interview with author. Telephone interview. Anaheim, CA. December 1, 8, 11, 2010 and April 26, 2011.

Muhammad, Akbar. "Muslims." FRONTLINE, PBS. May 9, 2002. http://www.pbs.org/wgbh/pages/frontline/shows/muslims/etc./script.html

Mohammed, Clarence Walker (Nephew). Interview with author. Telephone Interview. Anaheim, CA. January, 2008; December 8, 2009; January 17, 2010; February 10, 2010; August, 18, 2011; Personal Interview. Atlanta, GA. September 28, 2011; Telephone interview. October 3, 2011.

Mohammed, Burnsteen. Interview with author. Telephone interview. Anaheim, CA. May 6, 1982; March 19, 2001.

Mohammed, Elijah, Jr. Interview with author. Telephone interview. Macomb, Mississippi. April 22, 23, 2011; June 8, 9, 2012.

Mohammed, Haleemah (Granddaughter). Interview with author. Telephone Interview. Anaheim, CA. December 14, 2013.

Mohammed, Mother Ruby. Interview with author. Telephone interview. Anaheim, CA. August 19, 2010.

Mohammed, Nathaniel. Interview with author. Telephone interview. Big Lake, MN. August 19, 2010; December 1, 2, 5, 2010; April 8, 2011; July 18, 19, 2012; August 11, 2012; February 19, 2013.

Mohammed, Rayya. Interview with author. Personal interview. Sedalia, NC. April 30, 1983.

Mohammed, Imam W. Deen. Interview with author. Personal interview. Sedalia, NC. April 9, 1982; April 30, 1983. Email Correspondence. May 15, 2001; May, 2007.

Mohammed, Wali Akbar. Interview with author. Telephone interview. Anaheim, CA. December 14, 2010.

Muhammed, Queen Esther. Interview with author. Telephone interview. Clayton, Alabama.
August, 2011; September 8, 2011.

Muhammad, Ruquiyah

Nu'Mani, Aahira. Interview with author. Personal interview. New York, NY. May 23, 1982.

Porter, Carie (101 year old resident of Cordele, GA). Interview with author. Personal interview. Cordele, GA September 27,

2011.

Salaam, Marva. Interview with author. Telephone interview. Clayton, AL. August 12, 2011.

Shabazz, Dr. Abdul Aleem. Interview with author. Telephone interview. Anaheim, CA. December 28, 2010.

Shabazz, Della, wife of Dr. Abdul Aleem Shabazz (Lonnie Shabazz).

Shabazz, Elizabeth, widow of Jeremiah Shabazz

Sharif, Hasan. Interview with author. Telephone interview. Anaheim, CA. January 9, 2011; December 13, 2012.

Siddeeq, Mohammed. Interview with author. Telephone interview. Anaheim, CA. December 30, 2010.

Weaver, Erkstin. Interview with author. Telephone interview. Cordele, GA. October 18, 2012.

Websites

"The Ku Klux Klan." www.digitalhistory.uh.edu.

"The Ku Klux Klan." www.wikepedia.org.

"Red Summer -The 1916 Chicago Race Riots." www.encyclopediabritannica.com.

"The Rise and Fall of Jim Crow; The Ku Klux Klan." *PBS*. www.pbs.org.

www.amechurch.com.

www.britanica.com/EBchecked /topic/19996/American-Missionary-Association-AMA

www.newgeorgiaencyclopedia.org.

http://millercenter.org/president/mckinley/essays/

biography/4

Government Documents And Reports

Lucille Rosary v. Elijah Muhammad, Superior Court of Los Angeles, #D652479 (1964).

In the Matter of the Estate of Elijah Muhammad, Deceased, October 13, 1978

Mohammed, Clara Evans. FBI File # FOIPA # 1141893-00/190. March 19, 2010.

Mohammed, Elijah

U.S. Bureau of the Census. *Thirteen, Fourteenth and Fifteenth Censuses of the United States: Population (Michigan) 1910, 1920 and 1930, vols. 1, 2, and 3, Part 1*. Washington, D.C. Government Printing Office 1913, 1922, and 1932.

U.S. Bureau of the Census. *Thirteenth Census of the United States Taken in the Year 1910: Statistics for Georgia*. Washington, D.C.: Government Printing Office, 1913.

U.S. Bureau of the Census. *Historical Statistics of the United States: Colonial Times to 1970. Bicentennial Edition*. Washington, D.C.: Government Printing Office, 1975.

U. S. Department of State. Office of the Historian. *Spanish-American War*. 1898. http://history.state.gov/

U. S. Department of Commerce. Bureau of the Census. Population of the United States, 1910-1960.

Joint Center for Political Studies. *A Policy Framework for Racial Justice*. Washington, D.C., 1983.

Klein, Joel L. and Condoleezza Rice. *U.S. Education Reform and National Security*. Independent Task Force Report no. 68. Council on Foreign Relations. New York: 2012.

Moynihan, Daniel Patrick. *The Negro Family: The Case for National Action*. Washington, D.C.: U.S. Government Printing Office, 1965.

Plessy v. Ferguson, 163 U.S. 537 (1896)

Work Projects Administration. Georgia Writers' Project. *Drums and Shadows*. Georgia: The University of Georgia, 1940.

Special Reports

Department of Women's Studies at State University of New York (Albany: University Publication of America) CIS, Bethesda, MD.

Encyclopedia of Oklahoma History & Culture (Oklahoma Historical Society).

Franklin, John Hope and Scott Ellsworth, eds. *The Tulsa Race Riot: A Scientific, Historical and Legal Analysis.* Oklahoma City: Tulsa Race Riot Commission, 2000.

Minutes of National Conventions, Publications and Presidents Office Correspondence (University Publications of America, 1994).

Muhammad, Precious Rasheeda. "Muslims and the Making of America." (Los Angeles and Washington, D.C.: Muslim Public Affairs Council, 2013).

Brown v. Board: It's Impact on Education, and What It Left Undone. African-American Studies at the Woodrow Wilson Center #2, Washington, D.C., 2002.

Patterson, James T. *The Troubled Legacy of Brown v Board*. African-American Studies Woodrow Wilson Center #2, Washington, D.C., 2002.

Report of the Research Committee on Thomas Jefferson and Sally Hemings. Thomas Jefferson Foundation (Monticello: January, 2000).

Records of the National Association of Colored Women's Clubs 1895-1992.

Rosewood Victims v. State of Florida. *Special Masters Report of the Florida Legislature* (March 24, 1994).

Dissertations

Al-Kabi, Hatim Abdul Sahib. "The Nation of Islam." Diss., The University of Chicago. December, 1951.

Brackman, Harold David. "The Ebb and Flow of Conflict: A History Black-Jewish Relations Through 1900." Dissertation, University of California, Los Angeles, 1977.

Fanusie, Fatimah Abdul-Tawwab, "Fard Muhammad in Historical Context: An Islamic Thread in the American, Religious and Cultural Quilt." Dissertation, Howard University, 2008.

Rahman, Ajile Aisha Amatullah. "She Stood By His Side and At Times in His Stead: The Life and Legacy of Sister Clara Muhammad, First Lady of the Nation of Islam." Diss., Clark-Atlanta University. December, 1999.

Documentaries

"This Far by Faith" - *Episode 5: Inheritors of the Faith*, 2003. Reverend James H. Cone, The Architect of Black Liberation Theology.

EPILOGUE: "THAT THE SLAVE GIRL WILL GIVE BIRTH TO HER MISTRESS"

The life of Clara and Elijah Muhammad and the work of their son, Imam W. Deen Mohammed, illuminates a 7th-century prophecy that signifies an Islamic connection to a people who came from an Islamic past.[218] This essential prophecy, in a Hadith[219] regarded as the *Mother of the Sunnah*,[220] states in part that a sign of the *last days* is, "*That The Slave Girl Will Give Birth to Her Mistress.*"

In pondering this Hadith, it impressed me that *The Slave Girl* is a people – Muslim African Americans – and their birth is true human freedom. I discussed my thoughts with several Qur'anic scholars, authors, and teachers, including Imam(s) Ron El-Amin, Faheem Shuaib, Qasim Ahmed, and Dr. Akbar Muhammad (1933-2016), the last child of Clara and Elijah Muhammad; Emeritus Professor, State University New York, Binghamton; an alum of Al Azhar University, Cairo, Egypt and the University of Edinburg, Scotland. They listened attentively to my rationale and were surprised at my direction. Each challenged every hypothesis, raising thoughtful questions. I appreciated the conservations and written responses they shared. After several intense discussions with Dr. Akbar Muhammad, he did not discourage me, to my delight. Still, he cautioned that some scholars would not agree and I should be prepared to defend my position. Acknowledging various interpretations of this prophecy,[221] the author proposes the following:

This prophecy describes an unprecedented regeneration of a people who gave birth to themselves – by the authority of G-D – in their quest for true human freedom. That the human freedom they lost and found is The Qur'an and Al-Islam, their inheritance. The prophecy reads: *"That The Slave Girl Will Give Birth to Her Mistress" An talid al-ammatu rabbata-ha:*

> *The prophecy says that the Angel Jibreel* [222] */ Gabriel visited Muhammad the Prophet (PPBUH) to question him about three (3) things: 1) the Revelation of The Qur'an he was receiving; 2) his understanding of the principles of Al-Islam; and 3) the time of the last days.*
>
> *The Angel Jibreel said, Tell me about Al-Islam. Prophet Muhammad (PPBUH) said, Al-Islam is to testify that there is no G-D, but Allah and Muhammad is the Messenger of Allah; to perform the prayers, to pay the zakat (charity); to fast in Ramadan and to make the pilgrimage to the House (Ka'ba) if one is able to do so. The Angel Jibreel responded, You have spoken rightly. He then said, Tell me about Iman (faith). Prophet Muhammad (PPBUH) said, It is to believe in Allah, His angels, His Books, His Messengers, and the Last Day and to believe in divine destiny, both the good and evil thereof. Angel Jibreel said You have spoken rightly. He then said, Tell me about Ihsan (righteous action). Prophet Muhammad (PPBUH) responded, It is to worship Allah as though you see Him and though you see Him not, He truly sees you. Angel Jibreel said that is right. Now, tell me about the Hour [last days]. Prophet Muhammad (PPBUH) said The one questioned about it knows no more than the questioner. He said, then tell me about its signs. Prophet Muhammad (PPBUH) said, One of its signs is 'That the Slave Girl Will Give Birth to Her Mistress.' And you will see barefooted, naked, destitute herdsmen competing in constructing lofty buildings."* [223]

The clarity of this prophecy is in the Arabic language.

The word for slave is *abd* – a single slave. In this instance, *abd* is not used. Instead, it is *ammat* or *ummat*, which is plural and literally means, a community, a distinct nation, people, tribe, kinsfolk, etc. The tense – nouns and pronouns – are all feminine. Therefore, the accurate translation is not *master*, i.e. (That the slave girl will give birth to her master) as some have previously suggested but a *mistress*. The words for girl and mistress are both feminine and plural, thus representing a society or community, not individuals.

A girl is immature, has not reached maturity, and is dependent on others. A mistress is parallel to a master, mature and controlling one's circumstances. The definition of a slave is one who is oppressed, the property of or under the authority of another, and bound to serve that one [without appropriate compensation or the option of refusal].[224] Another definition of a *slave* is one held in bondage from one's full potential, be that potential physical freedom, emotional, intellectual, economic, or cultural freedom, or otherwise. The word *rabbata-ha* means nurtured from within (regenerating or rebirthing itself – with the permission of G-D) from one stage to a series of higher stages towards self-governance, rule.

Thus, the *slave girl* is a *community* of oppressed and/ or held in bondage from their full potential; immature in establishment, not fully developed. The *mistress* is a *community* that is mature, in charge of one's potential, exercising power, rule, and status over one's circumstances. The prophecy says the *slave girl* will generate birth within to become a community that will (*rabbata-ha*) nurture and self-govern into her full potential of power, rule, and status until she becomes the *mistress*, a mature community that is self-governing and in control of one's own circumstances.

The *slave girl* is the physical property of the mistress, is physically possessed by the mistress, but not spiritually or intellectually owned by the mistress. The *slave girl* is spiritually and intellectually owned by G-D / Allah and will inherit what the *mistress* possesses – not take away from – but inherit. She will inherit self-governance, power, rule, and status, everything denied as a result of enslavement. Why will the *slave girl community* inherit? She will inherit because of the justice and mercy of G-D/Allah, not simply because the *slave girl community* was oppressed. But more because of the *slave girl, the community* maintained her moral consciousness, her love of G-D, and her obedience to G-D amid oppression. She remained faithful to the inherent human nature – *fitra* – that G-D put in her. And even under oppression, she did not deviate from her moral foundation.

Thus, irrespective of the philosophical/ideological beginnings of the Nation of Islam, the majority of the members lived disciplined, moral lives and consistently worked for freedom, justice, and equality for their brothers and sisters. It is important to recall there was no institutional help for African people during their kidnap, enslavement, and forced religious conversion in the Americas from the early 1500s to 1930. No Jewish, Christian, or Muslim heads of religions, governments, or countries came to the aid of the Black man and woman in America for nearly 400 years.[225] Instead, each was complicit in the enslavement of those who are now known as African Americans.

This was a people solely dependent on The Creator, G-D Almighty. Consequently, when the son of Clara Muhammad became leader, he stated (on behalf of Muslim African Americans): "We are not to align with any foreign government Muslim or other, we only support the good they do. We are never to forget that no government came to our rescue..."[226] The only significant help Clara and her people received was from a single man, a mystic, W. D. Fard Muhammad, in 1930. He observed their circumstances, broke from his Ahmadiyya religious order, and constructed a methodology that came to be known as *The Lost Found Nation of Islam in the Wilderness of North America.* However, he did not come of his own volition; he was inspired by G-D, Allah, The Creator, and Lord of the Worlds to do so.

Regarded as the Saviour by people looking for prophetic

relief from mental, racial, and economic oppression, W. D. Fard Muhammad freed them from the *psychological slave masters' grip*. However, while imprisoned, Clara's husband, Elijah Muhammad, concluded that some of the methods promoted by W. D. Fard Muhammad stated in Supreme Wisdom Lessons[227] were violent and would not benefit his people. When released from prison, Elijah made a radical shift, eliminating any references to violence and the killing of four devils.[228] Members were forbidden to carry even a "penknife," and the focus of the *Lost Found Nation of Islam* was "Knowledge *of* Self" and "*Do For Self*" empowerment.

In 1930, the lens of history had not extended sufficiently for society to discern that *The Lost Found Nation of Islam in the Wilderness of North America* represented the *seedlings* of Al-Islam proper to a people to whom it was lost. The enslavement experience interrupted Black people from their previous life. Although that life was hollowed out of them during physical enslavement in the Americas, that hollowed vessel of a people possessed a genetic memory – a predisposition to the way of life of their ancestors – Muslims practicing Al-Islam.[229] This is why the story of the African-American generally, and Muslim African Americans specifically is like no other in human narration or record.[230]

Each movement to true human freedom for Black people was a progression towards the independent thinking of the Nation of Islam and ultimately towards The Qur'an. It began with enslaved ancestors – Muslims who led major slave rebellions and subsequent leaders who pointed out the contradictions between the oppression of Black people and the white racial Christianity as practiced by their oppressors. Leaders such as Nat Turner, David Walker, Frederick Douglass, Harriett Tubman, Sojourner Truth, Ida B. Wells, J.A. Rogers, Paul Robeson, and W. E. B. DuBois, among a host of others, raised substantive questions over decades. They sought justice within the Christian ideological framework. Unable to find it, several adopted Marxist ideology as a solution, as did Paul Robeson and

W. E. B. Dubois and revolutionaries and leaders of colonized countries.

The historical legacy of Al-Islam among African peoples of Andalusia, Timbuktu, and Songhai recalled by Edward Blyden[231] appeared to not invoke sufficient vision as a model solution to the spiritual and social problems among Black people in America. Unable to make the connection and having little firsthand knowledge of The Qur'an, notable Black leaders continued to be overwhelmed with appealing to white Christian America for mercy and justice, even though Blyden specifically said as early as 1887 that Al-Islam was better for the Negro than Christianity.[232] And Mahatma Gandhi made a similar statement to theologian Howard Thurman in the 1930s.

The prophecy *"That the Slave Girl Will Give Birth to Her Mistress"* is situated in the context of the *last days*. Islamic scholars assert that it does not denote the end of the physical world as often suggested. Instead, it represents the end of the man-made world of false ideologies and oppressive governments that repress human potential. The implication is that a new world based on truth will replace the one that is ending; a new world consistent with the created pattern G-D has designed for natural human development codified in Revelation (The Qur'an) and demonstrated in the lives of the Prophets, specifically the last Prophet, Muhammad ibn Abdullah, PPBUH. This prophecy was documented approximately 1,500 years ago and is recorded in sahih (sound) Hadith[233] literature.

Perhaps the most compelling proof of this prophecy is regeneration. The small group of early Muslims gave birth to their own leaders. Clara Muhammad taught her sons and daughters, and they taught their sons and daughters, and converts who became Muslim taught their children, etc. That regeneration came from within the circle of Muslims with a distinct generational evolution in intellectual thought and spiritual insight. Anchored in the commitment to help their people, the new Muslims studied, relied on their intelligence, addressed their needs, and advanced the Nation of Islam. This unprecedented period in history was influenced by Clara's role as wife to Elijah Muhammad, Mother to the Nation of Islam, and nurturer of her son, Imam W. Deen Mohammed.

Although aware of the traditional Muslim world and the importance of Islamic traditions, it was first important for this community of people to rely on Allah/G-D to help them break the psychological hold white supremacy had on their intelligence. Once free, they could develop from their own souls a life that addressed their unique intellectual, spiritual and cultural needs. Then with the knowledge of The Qur'an and the traditions of Prophet Muhammad, PPBUH, they could strive for human excellence, and fulfill the prophecy and promises G-D / Allah made to Prophet Abraham/Ibrahim, peace be upon him.

As the early Muslims on the Arabian Peninsula cannot separate Muhammad the Prophet, PPBUH, and the growth of Al-Islam from Khadijah bint Khuwaylid, wife and mother of his children, so Muslim African Americans cannot separate their evolution from Clara Evans Muhammad, Elijah Muhammad, and their progeny, Imam W. Deen Mohammed, even if many of these Muslim African Americans were not a part of the Nation of Islam or a follower of Imam W. Deen Mohammed. The unprecedented work and sacrifices of the early Muhammad family and the early Muslim members laid the foundation for Al-Islam in America, from which all Muslims have benefited, and the general American public as well It all began with the loving patient perseverance of a mother searching for sustenance to save her family. As a result, Muslim African Americans represent hope for America and for the Muslim world. Their 400-year sojourn in America has qualified them to carry the spirit of The Qur'an. Now,they need only to live up to their potential.

We are forever indebted to the Mother of the Nation, Clara Evans Muhammad. She lives in the Clara Muhammad Schools and in the generations of men and women who model obedience to G-D and the best of their human excellence. We thank her and honor her. Her son once told an audience overwhelmed with challenges, *"Hold on to the spirit of Clara Muhammad."*

ACKNOWLEDGMENTS

Special thanks for the invaluable contributions of Elijah Muhammad, Jr., Hasan Sharif, son of Ethel Muhammad Sharrieff, Halimah Muhammad-Ali, daughter of Lottie Rayya Muhammad, and Elijah Muhammad, 3rd son of Herbert Muhammad. And a special debt of gratitude to Harriet Muhammad-Abu Bakr, former daughter-in-law of Clara and Ruqaiyah Muhammad- Farrar, granddaughter of Clara and daughter of Emmanuel Muhammad.

In Detroit, pioneers Burnsteen Mohammed, Juanita Shakir, and Mary'am T. Muhammad provided insightful information on the first generation of Muslims in the *Lost Found Nation of Islam*. They were most kind. Special appreciation to Nasir Muhammad, Black Mecca Tours, Atlanta, Georgia. To Imams Faheem Shuaibe and Ron El-Amin, Mario Abdus-Salaam Ahmad (ra), Sharif Abdus Salaam, Imam Usamah Ansari and Imam Darnell Kariem. And to Imam Qasim Ahmed for his Qur'anic insight and Agieb Bilal, for his incomparable intellect and assistance, thank you.

To the librarians without whose support this project would have been exceeding more difficult, thank you.

Finally to the Sisters, Muslim women who at times picked me up stood me up, raised me up, and covered my back, regardless: Amatullah Okapu Sharief (ra), Jameelah Malik, Aaliyah Muhammad- Sacramento, Khadijah Mahdi, Dr. Aisha Kareem, Dr. Joyce King, Dr. Sally Kwon, Dr. Dena Amar, Rawiyah Khatib, Rasheedah Abdul Hameed, Adilah Kariem, Safiyya Sharif, Hajjah Judy Moussa, Amatullah Alaji Sabrie, Tauheedah Williams, Hajjah Aaliyah AbdulWali, The Breaux-Abdur Rahman Trust, Aaliyah Akbar, Abrafi Sanyika, Joan Sabree-Faqir, Nafeesah Mustafa Rasheed, Aidah Aaliyah Rasheed, Zakiyyah Nu'Man, Ameenah Mahdee, Shahidah Shukri, Nadina Yasin, Simin Omar, Mrs. Bushra Aslam, Mrs. Rahana Abdul Wahab, Mrs. Basri Aktar,

Mrs. Rashida Syed, Imrose Salihue, Ayesha Mustafaa, Basima Mousa, Khadijah Sharif Drinkard, Asia Sharif Clark, Ameedah Sharif, and Tayyaba Anis. You are the best Sisters I have ever known and are a blessing in my life. Thank you.

And special thanks to John and Alice Coltrane for their brilliant, inspiring formulations that reach for The Creator and take our souls along in the process.

It was enlightening and humbling to witness the love for Clara Evans Muhammad and the Muslim experience in America. With great appreciation to the countless pioneers who laid the foundation, to those who continue to build and live with integrity, for every word shared, every photograph and artifact sent, and for every prayer made on behalf of this effort, thank you. Alhumdulillah - Praise Be To Allah!

ABOUT THE AUTHOR

Dr. Zakiyyah was a devout servant of Allah. Her love of Allah, His Prophet (PBUH), and Al-Islam was reflected in all that she did. Her intellectual approach to teaching Al-Islam was exceptional, and her undeniable scholarship will always be remembered.

She earned a Doctorate in Education from Teachers College, Columbia University, New York, and wrote the first dissertation on Islamic Schools in America. An internationally recognized expert in Islamic education and Muslim women, she was a teacher, principal, professor of education. She was appointed Director of Education for Clara Muhammad Schools by Imam W. Deen Mohammed.

She lectured at Stanford University, the University of Chicago, California State University-Sacramento, DePaul University, and the International Institute of Islamic Thought. She also was a social commentary columnist for the Muslim Journal and documented the educational evolution of the Muslim African-American community.

A former research associate to Dr. C. Eric Lincoln, and an affiliated scholar at Howard University under the direction of Dr. Sulayman Nyang, Dr. Zakiyyah presented at the Woodrow Wilson International Center for Scholars, Georgetown University, and at the Association for the Study of African-American Life and History, ASALAH. She published in the Journal of Negro Education, Journal on Religion and Education, Encyclopedia of African-American Education, Muslim Education Quarterly, and the American Educational Research Association's Black Education.

Dr. Zakiyyah led an exemplary life and was an inspiration and support for all who knew her. She was a mother, a sister, a teacher. She will be remembered for her generosity of spirit, kind nature, an understanding heart, incredible acts of charity, and loyalty as a friend and relative.

AFTERWORD

It has been a labor of love to bring this manuscript into the hands of the reader. Dr. Zakiyyah Muhammad founded the Institute of Muslim American Studies (IMAS) in 2014 to document the contributions of Muslim African Americans to American culture, develop the field of Muslim American Studies as an academic discipline, and continue the Muslim African-American historical legacy of Interfaith Dialogue.

We lost this incredible scholar in June 2019. However, the board of IMAS remains committed to sharing her lifelong project of documenting the life of an incredible pioneer, Sr. Clara Muhammad. Dr. Zakkiyah left us with a heavy trust, a manuscript filled with the years she dedicated to researching Sr. Clara's life and time spent carefully writing. This book contains her thoughts and opinions, both commonly agreed upon and controversial. We have chosen to deliver her words to the reader, leaving as much of her original language as possible.

I am deeply grateful to John Woodford for his contributions in editing and writing the foreword to this volume. I also wanted to share my extreme gratitude to the board members Br. Agieb Bilal, Sr. Jameelah Malik and Sr. Aaliyah Muhammad. Additionally, I wanted to thank Mina Ahmad-Crosby for her editing and publishing support. We hope Sr. Clara's journey inspires you through triumph and turmoil and that you gain a deeper understanding of the impact her life had on so many Americans.

Judy Moussa
President,
Institute of Muslim American Studies

END NOTES

[1] Referred to as colored after Emancipation, W. E. B. Dubois suggested Negro in the late 19th century; it was embraced by Marcus Garvey. With the introduction of the Lost Found Nation of Islam in 1930, Elijah Muhammad championed Black as the choice of identity. As the new leader of the Nation of Islam in 1975, Imam W. Deen Mohammed said, "Black leadership used the term Afro-American as if they were afraid to say the whole word (African)." He personally had reservations with the term "African" because the continent was named by someone other than its native people. He offered the term "Bilalian" but stated if our people didn't want to accept it, they should at least have the courage to say the complete word "African". In 1988, "African American" was promoted by the Rev. Jesse Jackson, although he was hardly the first to use the term. Throughout history, "Black" was used in a derogatory manner until the Lost Found Nation of Islam in the 1930s used the term denoting racial pride. Today, many still use the term Black for good and ill.

[2] What Imam W.D. Muhammad Taught," by Agieb Bilal, *Muslim Journal.*

[3] Telephone interview with Nathaniel Muhammad, December 1, 2010.

[4] Muhammad, Zakiyyah, Ummology: The Study of Mother, The Original Feminine Principle. Unpublished Manuscript.

[5] Ibid.

[6] This concept was articulated by Imam W. Deen Mohammed and based upon various revelations from The Qur'an. See: Qur'an Al Rum (The Roman Empire) 30:30.

[7] Mother Leadership is a concept advanced by the son of Clara Muhammad, Imam W. Deen Mohammed.

[8] Williams, Delores S., Sisters in the Wilderness: The Challenge of Womanist G-D-Talk, Orbis Books, Maryknoll, New York, 1993. p. 235.

[9] Written by composer William E. Barton, 1899. It is reported

someone said of the song, "It is the saddest and most beautiful song of slavery".

[10] Lesson #1 Question #11 from The Supreme Wisdom Lessons by W. D. Fard Muhammad given to Elijah Muhammad for the Lost-Found Nation of Islam in North America.

[11] Mueller, Denis and Ellis, Deb (Video 1990) "The FBI's War on Black America"

[12] Sahib, Hatim Abdul. The Nation of Islam. The University of Chicago, 1951 p. 70.

[13] Muhammad's University of Islam Vol 2 (1963) https://issuu.com/muhammadspeaks/docs/uoi-1963

[14] Christopher Manning, "African Americans", Encyclopedia of Chicago, http://www.encyclopedia/chicagohistory.org/pages/27

[15] Personal interview with Lottie Rayya Muhammad, Sedalia, North Carolina, 1982.

[16] Ibid.

[17] Ross, Rosetta. Witnessing and Testifying, Black Women, Religion and Civil Rights. Fortress Press, Minneapolis, MN, 2003, p. 149.

[18] Ibid.

[19] Lincoln, C. Eric. The Black Muslims in America. Beacon Press, Boston, 1961, p. 32, 126, 127. See also: Rashid, Hakim and Zakiyyah Muhammad. The Sister Clara Muhammad Schools: Pioneers in the Development of Islamic Education in America. Journal of Negro Education, 61:2, 1992.

[20] Woodson, Carter G. The Mis-Education of the Negro, 1933

[21] Ibid, p. 134.

[22] Ibid, p. 138.

[23] Ibid, p. 144.

[24] Telephone interview with Khalilah Camacho Ali.

[25] Lincoln, C. Eric. The Black Muslims in America. Beacon Press, Boston, 1961, p. 250.

[26] DuBois, W.E.B. "Does the Negro Need Separate Schools?" 4 Journal of Negro Education, p. 329, July, 1935.

[27] Quote from Nicholas Lemann author of The Promised Land.

[28] Clegg 3rd, Claude Andrew. An Original Man - The Life and Times of Elijah Muhammad. New York: St. Martin's Press, 1997

[29] Evanzz, Karl. The Messenger – The Rise and Fall of Elijah Muhammad. New York: Pantheon Books, 1999.

[30] Detroit study of Pioneers

[31] Beynon, Erdmann Doane. "The Voodoo Cult Among Negro Migrants in Detroit." American Journal of Sociology 43, no. 6 (May, 1938): 894-907. University of Chicago Press. p. 905.

[32] Bible, Malachi 4:5.

[33] Encyclopedia of Chicago 2004 The Newberry Library; See also The Electronic Encyclopedia of Chicago, 2005; Chicago Historical Society.

[34] Ibid.

[35] Ibid.

[36] Comment Clara made to her parents before she eloped with Elijah.

[37] Milwaukee Pioneers in the Nation of Islam, 2014. YouTube, https://www.youtube.com/watch?v=3BCmDgZo1n8

[38] Message to the Blackman in America, p. 257.

[39] Statement from Imam W. Deen Mohammed

[40] w Harlem Riot of 1935, See: http://www.blackpast.org/aah/harlem-riot-1935

[41] Interview Lottie Rayya Muhammad, Sedalia, North Carolina, 1982.

[42] Ibid.

[43] Telephone interview, with Elijah Muhammad, Jr., April 22, 2011.

[44] Ibid.

[45] Interview Lottie Rayya Muhammad, Sedalia, North Carolina, 1982.

[46] Telephone interview, with Elijah Muhammad, Jr., April 22, 2011.

[47] Ibid.

[48] Ibid.

[49] Ibid.

[50] Ibid.

[51] Ibid.

[52] Ibid.

[53] Interview with Hasan Sharief, Anaheim, CA.

[54] Muhammad, Benjamin Ilyas (formerly Benjamin X Mitchell) The Early Days of Al-Islam in Washington, D.C., (1935-1942). Washington, D.C. 1994. p. 21.

[55] Mitchell, Benjamin X. The Early Days of Al-Islam in Washington, DC. Washington, D.C. 1994, p. 21-22

[56] Interview Lottie Rayya Muhammad, Sedalia, North Carolina, 1982.

[57] http://www.mlive.com/news/detroit/index.ssf/2010/08/early_nation_of_islam_document.html

[58] https://www.ha.com/heritage-auctions-press-releases-and-news/nation-of-islam-archive-elijah-muhammad-personal-items-offered-at-heritage-auctions.s?releaseId=3177

[59] Established in Baltimore, Maryland, 1885 to gain social justice for Black People. They were responsible for establishing the first colored schools and enabling the students to be taught by colored teachers and have colored principals. They also enabled the first black lawyer and opened the University of Maryland Law School for Black people. They are referred to as the second NAACP.
See: https://en.wikipedia.org/wiki/Brotherhood_of_Liberty

[60] Founded in 1932, Chicago as a back to African effort to repatriate Liberia. It was believed to have been supported by the Black Dragon Society of communist Japan and Satakata Takahashi.

[61] Clegg III, Claude Andrew. An Original Man, The Life and Times of Elijah Muhammad. St. Martin's Press, NY, 1997. p. 85.

[62] Benjamin Ilyas Muhammad (formerly Benjamin X Mitchell) The Early Days of Al-Islam in Washington, D.C., (1935-1942). Washington, D.C. 1994. p. 19.

[63] Ibid, p. 22.

[64] Interview Lottie Rayya Muhammad

[65] Ibid.

[66] Ibid.

[67] Telephone interview with Elijah Muhammad, Jr. Also clarification was made in a public address by Elijah Muhammad, Jr.

[68] Interview Lottie Rayya Muhammad, 1982

[69] Milwaukee Pioneers in the Nation of Islam, 2014.
See YouTube, https://www.youtube.com/watch?v=3BCmDgZo1n8

[70] Interview with Ruqaiyah Muhammad-Farrar

[71] Interview with Carl Omar.

[72] Telephone interview with Darnell Kariem.

[73] Telephone interview with Elijah Muhammad, Jr.

[74] Statement made by Elijah Muhammad.

[75] Telephone interview with Elijah Muhammad, Jr.

[76] Ibid.

[77] Ibid.

[78] Ibid.

[79] Telephone interview with Elijah Muhammad, Jr.

[80] Strong, S.M. (1946). Review of Black Metropolis. American Sociological Review, 11 (2), 240-241.

[81] Smith v. Allwright, 1944. See: https://www.law.cornell.edu/supremecourt/text/321/649

[82] Albert Einstein, The Negro Question, 1946. See: http://

www.onbeing.org/program/albert-einstein-the-negro-question-1946.

[83] Ibid.

[84] Interview with Nathaniel Muhammad.

[85] Telephone Interview Khalilah Kamaacho Ali.

[86] Clegg III, Claude Andrew. An Original Man, The Life and Times of Elijah Muhammad. St. Martin's Press, NY, 1997.

[87] Interview with Darnell Kariem

[88] Comments from Professor Jamil Diab relayed by Imam Darnell Kariem, Imam W. Deen Mohammed and others.

[89] Ibid.

[90] Interview with Darnell Kariem

[91] Qur'an, Ali Imran (the Family of Imran) 3:36.

[92] Telephone interview with Ruquiyyah Muhammad-Farrar – Anaheim, CA to Atlanta, Georgia

[93] The answer to Question #14 of Lesson #1 of the Supreme Wisdom, What is the meaning of MGT&GCC?

[94] Quote from Supreme Wisdom, Nation of Islam

[95] From Message to the Blackman in America

[96] Edward E. Curtis, IV. Black Muslim Religion in the Nation of Islam, 1960-1975. Chapel Hill University of North Carolina Press, 2006. p. 29.

[97] Bayyinah S. Jeffries. A Nation Can Rise No Higher Than Its Women. Lexington Books, New York, 2014, p.61.

[98] "Black Women Invented the Feminist Movement," Black Enterprise, March 19, 2015.

[99] Telephone Interview with Hasan Sharief, Chicago, IL / Anaheim, CA, January 9, 2011.

[100] Ibid.

[101] Telephone Interview, Hasan Sharif, January 9, 2011.

[102] Ibid.

[103] The Washington Afro-American, "Stress on Equality Brings Shift to Mohammedanism", July 28, 1945, p. 8.

[104] Ibid.

[105] Richard Brent Turner, Islam in the African-American Experience. Indiana University Press, Bloomington, 1997, p. 171.

[106] Telephone interview with Hasan Sharief.

[107] Minister Wallace 1959, Introduced by Malcolm X (Imam W Deen Mohammed @ 26 yrs) https://www.youtube.com/watch?v=47KvJpNwXSs

[108] Taylor Branch, Pillar of Fire, p. 15-20.

[109] W. D. Muhammad, "Impact of Islam on Muslim Women." Mr. Muhammad Speaks, September 1960, p. 31-32.

[110] Ibid.

[111] Telephone interview with Della Shabazz, Atlanta, Georgia, August 29, 2017.

[112] Muhammad, Elijah, Message to the Blackman in America, p. 192

[113] Interview with Nathaniel Muhammad

[114] Telephone interview with Tauheedah Mahmound Fard

[115] *Brown v. Board: Its Impact on Education, and What it Left Undone.* Woodrow Wilson International Center for Scholars, Division of United States Studies Washington, D.C. 2002.

[116] Telephone interview, Wali Akbar Muhammad, Atlanta, Georgia.

[117] Ibid.

[118] Telephone interview with Ruquiyah Muhammad.

[119] Ibid.

[120] Elijah Muhammad Dead: Black Muslim Leader 77, Special to The New York Times, February 26, 1975. http://www.nytimes.com/learning/general/onthisday/bday/1007.html.

[121] Emmanuel Muhammad, article in Muhammad Speaks

[122] Interview with Clarence Walker Muhammad, Atlanta, Georgia

[123] Baldwin, James. The Fire Next Time. New York: Dell Publishing Co., Inc. 1962, p. 72.

[124] Interview with Fern Genobia Tauheedah Mahmoud.

[125] Telephone interview with Minister Louis Farrakhan, Chicago, Illinois/Anaheim, CA August 5, 2010.

[126] Personal and Telephone interview with Clarence Walker Muhammad, Nephew, Atlanta, GA and from Anaheim, CA to Atlanta, Georgia.

[127] Interview Imam Darnell Kariem

[128] Telephone interview with Ruquiyyah Muhammad-Farrar Anaheim, California to Atlanta, Georgia and Halimah Muhammad-Ali, Atlanta, Georgia.

[129] Telephone interview with Minister Louis Farrakhan from Anaheim, California to Chicago, Illinois, August 5, 2010.

[130] Interview Khalilah Comacho Ali.

[131] Telephone interview with Shakeelah Hassan, Anaheim, CA to Chicago, Illinois, 2015.

[132] Ibid. See: http://frequencies.ssrc.org/2011/09/20/shakeela-hassan/

[133] Telephone interview with Hasan Sharif, son of Ethel and Raymond Sharrieff.

[134] Ibid.

[135] Telephone interview with Hasan Sharif, son of Ethel and Raymond Sharrieff.

[136] Telephone interview with Elizabeth Shabazz

[137] The Autobiography of Malcolm X, Random House, New York, 1964, p. 342

[138] Telephone interview, Elijah Muhammad, Jr., April 22, 2011.

[139] Telephone interview with Hasan Sharif, son of Ethel and Raymond Sharrieff.

[140] Ibid.

[141] Ibid.

[142] Ibid.

[143] Interview with Nathaniel Muhammad

[144] See: *Lucille Rosary v. Elijah Muhammad*, Superior Court of Los Angeles, #D652479 (1964), "Order to Show Cause," July 6, 1964, 3. See also: https://archive.org/stream/FBI-Elijah-Muhammad/105-HQ-24822-12_djvu.txt

[145] *In the Matter of the Estate of Elijah Muhammad, Deceased*, October 13, 1978, testimony of Emmanuel Muhammad, 2-26.

[146] Ibid, Note 40, 8.

[147] Personal and telephone interview with Harriet Muhammad AbuBakr, Atlanta, GA.

[148] Telephone interview with Delores Diamiah Jordan,

[149] Telephone interview with Hasan Muhammad Sharrieff,

[150] Telephone interview with Ruquiyyah Muhammad-Farrar Anaheim, California to Atlanta, Georgia

[151] Telephone interview with Ruquiyyah Muhammad-Farrar – Anaheim, CA to Atlanta, Georgia

[152] W. D. Muhammad. "Impact of Islam on Muslim Women". *Mr. Muhammad Speaks*, September, 1960, 31-32.

[153] Reverend James H. Cone, "This Far By Faith" PBS Documentary. See video https://www.youtube.com/watch?v=TTRDwUjeMEw

[154] Telephone interview with Elizabeth Shabazz, Philadelphia, PA

[155] Ibid.

[156] Ibid.

[157] Abdullah Yusuf Ali translation of Qur'an, Chapter An Nissa (The

Women) 4:3

[158] See Qur'an Al Baqarah, Chapter 2: 228.

[159] Telephone interview, Elijah Muhammad, Jr. 9/19/17

[160] Interview with Nathaniel Muhammad

[161] Telephone interview, Elijah Muhammad, Jr. 9/19/17

[162] Telephone interview with Herbert, Jr. (Jesus) Muhammad

[163] Telephone interview with Minister Louis Farrakhan

[164] Statement from Ruqaiyah Muhammad-Farrar.

[165] See: The Prophetic Biography: Sirah of Ibnu Hisham. 'Abd Al Malik Ibn Hisham. Dar Al-Kotob Al-ilmiyah, Beirut, Lebanon, 1971, p. 651.

[166] Ibid.

[167] Ibid.

[168] Comments from Imam W. Deen Mohammed, *The Honorable Elijah Muhammad and the Dishonorable Elijah Muhammad.* Chicago Community Night, 1977.

[169] Personal and telephone interview with Harriet Muhammad Abubakr

[170] Ibid.

[171] Ibid.

[172] Ibid.

[173] See Al Qur'an, Al A'raf (The Heights) 7:172.

[174] Statement from Imam W. Deen Mohammed

[175] See: "This Far By Faith" https://mail.google.com/mail/u/0/#inbox/1632e1e91420f85f?projector=1

[176] Statement by Clara confirmed by Imam W. Deen Mohammed and all family members.

[177] Interview with Nathaniel Muhammad

[178] Interview with Rayya Muhammad, Sedalia, North Carolina, 1982.

[179] Ibid.

[180] Telephone interview with Agieb Bilal 4/29/17.

[181] Telephone interview with Geneva Walker Muhammad, wife of Clarence Walker Muhammad, Nephew of Clara Muhammad, Atlanta, Georgia, September 9, 2017.

[182] Halimah Muhammad-Ali presentation at American Islamic Heritage Museum, July, 2017.

[183] Telephone interview, Halimah Muhammad-Ali.

[184] Affirmative Action was first introduced in 1961 by President John F. Kennedy to redress discrimination against African Americans that persisted irrespective of civil rights laws and constitutional

guarantees. President Lyndon Baines Johnson further developed programs to support it.

[185] Telephone interview with Minister Louis Farrakhan, Chicago, Illinois/Anaheim, CA August 5, 2010.

[186] Telephone interview with Shakeelah Hassan, Chicago, Illinois.

[187] Interview with Nathaniel Muhammad

[188] Telephone interview, Minister Louis Farrakhan, Chicago, Illinois/ Anaheim, CA August 5, 2010.

[189] Telephone interview, Hafeesah Al Uqdah, Anaheim, California to Los Angeles, California

[190] Ibid.

[191] Telephone interview with Elizabeth Shabazz, from Anaheim, CA to Philadelphia, PA

[192] Telephone interview with Hasan Sheriff.

[193] Interview Lottie Rayya Muhammad

[194] Interview Imam W. Deen Mohammed

[195] Ibid.

[196] Statement from Lottie Rayya Muhammad, Sedalia, North Carolina.

[197] Statement from Hasan Sharif

[198] Ibid.

[199] Statement from Lottie Rayya Muhammad, Sedalia, North Carolina.

[200] Statement from Imam W. Deen Mohammed on The Legacy of Clara Muhammad

[201] Interview with Dr, Shakeelah Hassan

[202] *Rose Against the Wind: A Biography of Queen Esther Muhammed, Muslim American* Pioneer by Marva Salimah Salaam, P.O. Box 314, Clayton, AL 36016-0314 (334) 775-8247.

[203] Marva Salimah Salaam, telephone interview, Clayton, Alabama, October 4, 2017.

[204] *The Nation of Islam*, Dissertation, The University of Chicago, December, 1951 by Hatim A. Sahib.

[205] Luqman in The Qur'an, Chapter 31, verse 13, 14, 15. Abdullah Yusuf Ali Translation.

[206] Ibid.

[207] Lecture of Imam W Deen Mohammed,

[208] Akhenaten - meaning "living spirit of Aten" - known before the fifth year of his reign as Amenhotep IV (sometimes given its Greek form, Amenophis IV, and meaning Amun is Satisfied), was a Pharaoh of the Eighteenth dynasty of Egypt who ruled for 17 years and died

perhaps in 1336 BC or 1334 BC. Also see: https://en.wikipedia.org/wiki/Akhenaten

[209] Khadijah means, one who comforts.

[210] See: Muhammad's Companions Volume 1 by Laleh Bakhtiar

[211] See the full 1980 Resolution of the ABP in their archives and in Chains and Images of Psychological Slavery, New Mind Productions, New Jersey, 1984,

[212] Ibid.

[213] Ibid.

[214] Journey into America: The Challenge of Islam 2010'

[215] Branch, T. (2010). The Clinton Tapes: Wrestling History in the White House. United Kingdom: Simon & Schuster UK.

[216] Chiara Lubich: *The Essential Writings*, New City Press Hyde Park, NY, 2007, p. 345.

[217] Haberman, Joshua O. Senior Rabbi Emeritus, Washington Hebrew Congregation, July, 1992.

[218] Sylvian Dioff, Servants of Allah. There exists credible evidence that approximately 40% of enslaved Africans were Muslim from the west coast of Africa. See UNESCO – Africa from the Twelfth to Sixteenth Century Volume IV and Africa from the Sixteenth to Eighteenth Century, Volume V.

[219] Hadith literally means a report or account. It is a collection of reports of the words, actions and habits of Muhammad ibn Abdullah, the last Prophet who revealed The Qur'an, prayers and peace be upon him.

[220] A 7th century prophecy which is part of a Hadith of Prophet Muhammad (PPBUH) regarded as "the Mother or Core of the Sunnah." It is so regarded because it was in response to the Prophet being questioned by Jabreel, (the Angel Gabriel) regarding his understanding of Al-Islam and the time of the last days. To see the entire hadith go to: https://sunnah.com/nawawi40/2 It was narrated on the authority of Umar Ibn al-Khattab, recorded on the authority of Abu Huraira and compiled by Al Bukhari in Volume 1:47 of Sahih Al-Bukhari. It was later recorded in in Forty Hadith – An Anthology of the Sayings of The Prophet Muhammad (saws) by Al-Nawawi. Sautul Islam Publications, Inc. Princeton, NJ. Hadith # 2. Also see: *Servants of Allah: African Muslims Enslaved in The* Americas by Sylviane A. Diouf. New York University Press, 1998.

[221] Scholars have historically agreed there are varied interpretations of this prophecy. Explanations of the forty essential sayings known

as Commentary on the Forty Hadith of Al Nawawi by Jamaal al-Din M. Zarabozo suggests several meanings. One popularly espoused translation is, "When a woman will give birth to her master" offering two interpretations.

1. In the "last days" children will disrespect their mothers and rule over them.

2. Women impregnated by oppressors (from war, slavery, etc.) will bear children who will favor their fathers who will rule over their mothers as slaves.

A translation of the prophecy in Lanes Lexicon reads, "So that the female shall bring forth him who will become her master." The immediate problem with this translation is that the noun and pronoun are feminine in the construction Rabbata-ha thus the correct translation is not master _or_ mistress as listed in Lanes, but definitely _mistress_. The meaning of Rabbatun is "a large assembly or a group, thus it can be translated as "her large assembly or group". Societies and cities are always feminine.

[222] The Arabic name for the angel Gabriel.

[223] A part of a Hadith, recorded by Al - Bukhari and Muslim. Saying of Prophet Muhammad (PPBUH) narrated on the authority of Umar Ibn al-Khattab. Later compiled by Al-Bukhari and recorded in Forty Hadith – An Anthology of the Sayings of The Prophet Muhammad (saws) by Al-Nawawi. Sautul Islam Publications, Inc. Princeton, NJ. Hadith # 2. This Hadith is regarded as "the Mother or Core of the Sunnah." For the entire hadith see: https://sunnah.com/nawawi40/2 Also see: _Servants of Allah: African Muslims Enslaved in The_ Americas by Sylviane A. Diouf New York University Press, 1998.

[224] Random House Dictionary, Classic Edition, New York, 1983 p. 849.

[225] For the last 150 years of Jim Crow and the struggle for equality, the historical record shows no significant help from either of these groups although some individuals may have voiced concerns towards the last 25 years.

[226] From "What the Imam Taught Us"; Principles of Imam W. Deen Mohammed's Leadership by Agieb Bilal. Based on a telephone conference call with Imam W. Deen Mohammed from Sharjah, UAE to Chicago, Illinois, Ramadan, October, 2006.

[227] Lesson #1 - Question # 10 reads: Why did Muhammad and any Muslim murder the devil? What is the Duty of each Muslim in regards to four devils? What Reward does a Muslim receive by presenting the four devils at one time? Answer: Because he is One Hundred Percent wicked and will not keep and obey the Laws of Islam. His ways and

actions are like a snake of the grafted type. So Muhammad learned that he could not reform the devils, so they had to be murdered. All Muslims will murder the devil they know he is a snake and, also, if he be allowed to live, he would sting someone else. Each Muslim is required to bring four devils. And by bringing and presenting four at one time, his Reward is a button to wear on the lapel of his coat. Also, a free transportation in the Holy City (Mecca) to see Brother Muhammad.

[228] Ibid.

[229] This concept was raised by Imam W. Deen Mohammed.

[230] Mazrui, Ali A. "The Dual Memory, Genetic and Factual." *Transition Exchange*, no. 57 (Indiana University Press, 1992): 134-146; Edward Baptist "The Half Has Not Been Told", 2014; Dr. Mordecai Johnson, "The Faith of the American Negro", commencement address to Harvard University, 1922; Encyclopedia Britannica: Early Modern Plantation Slavery, pp 860-63; Macropedia, Volume 9 and 16, Chicago, IL, 1973-74; Slave Rebellions: U.S. and Slave Trade, pp. 266-267; Gunnar Myrdal, An American Dilemma: The Negro Problem and Modern Democracy, 1944.

See also: Lincoln, C. Eric, The Black Muslims in America.

[231] See Edward Blyden, *Christianity, Islam and the Negro Race*.

[232] Ibid.

[233] Hadith is a compilation of the sayings of Muhammad, the Last Prophet (PPBUH). They are of primarily three types: Sahih – strong, moderate and weak.